THE BOY LAMA

THE BOY LAMA

VICKI MACKENZIE

1817

Harper & Row, Publishers, San Francisco

New York, Grand Rapids, Philadelphia, St. Louis
London, Singapore, Sydney, Tokyo

PHOTO CREDITS

Robin Bath page 1 *top*, page 5 *bottom*, page 10 *top* & *bottom*, page 11, page 12 *top*; Thomas Begley page 9 *bottom*; Buddha House, Adelaide page 13 *bottom*; Andrew Byne page 4 *bottom*; Ricardo de Aratanha page 6 *bottom*, page 7; Sue Emonson page 12 *bottom*; Terry Fincher page 15, page 16 *bottom*; Dieter Kratzer page 1 *bottom*; Vicki Mackenzie page 5 *top*, page 14 *bottom*; Catherine Mackwood page 16 *top*; Janne Nicholls page 13 *top*; T. H. Parr / The Newark Museum page 4 *top*; Max Redlich page 8 *bottom*, page 9 *top*; Lama Zopa Rinpoche page 6 *top*; Ruth Sonam page 3 *top*; Chuck Thomas page 1 *bottom*; Vajrapani Centre, California page 14 *top*

FIRST U.S. EDITION PUBLISHED BY HARPER & ROW IN 1989.
Originally published in England by Bloomsbury Publishing Ltd.

Library of Congress Cataloging-in-Publication Data

Mackenzie, Vicki.
    The Boy Lama / Vicki Mackenzie. — 1st U.S. ed.
        p.   cm.
    Reprint. Originally published: Bloomsbury Pub., 1988.
    ISBN 0-06-250558-0
    1. Lamas — Biography 2. Thubten Yeshe, 1935– . 3. Hita, Osel.
4. Reincarnation — Biography.   I Title.
BQ7920.M33 1989
294.3'923'0924 — dc 19
[B]   89-45231
                                             CIP

89 90 91 92 93   10 9 8 7 6 5 4 3 2 1

May all sentient beings
be free from suffering and its cause.
May all sentient beings achieve true happiness.

— Tibetan Buddhist dedication

ACKNOWLEDGEMENTS

I would very much like to thank Lama Thubten Yeshe, Lama Tenzin Osel Rinpoche and Lama Zopa Rinpoche, without whom this book would have been impossible.
For their kindness and co-operation, I am also greatly indebted to Maria Torres Crespo, Paco Hita Garcia and family; all Kopan residents; all Vajrapani Centre residents; all at Wisdom Publications; and Robin Bath.

CONTENTS

INTRODUCTION

The morning was particularly bleak. Horizontal rain lacerated the slate-grey waves sloshing against my houseboat moored with military precision alongside the other floating homes on London's Chelsea Embankment. The boat had been my proud possession for just three months; 86 feet of Thames barge converted to an astonishing degree of modern convenience. But on this Saturday morning in October 1986 the weather mirrored my mood.

My surroundings, with their ever-changing play of light upon water and the dance of the tides, usually filled me with a quiet joy and a maverick sense of satisfaction at having dared the unconventional, but on this particular morning, life seemed especially glum. To be honest, my personal gloominess only reflected a far bigger, less delineated but more pervasive dissatisfaction, which the move to the new address, for all its romantic overtones, hadn't entirely dispelled. I wasn't sure what it was. A Baudelairean-type *ennui* perhaps, at the essential hollowness of life.

By rights, there should have been no complaints. My life was successful, privileged, comfortable, diverse. I had travelled to many lands, had a lot of adventures, learnt many things. My career as a national journalist had for the past 18 years offered a rich smorgasbord of challenge, fun, education and crisis. But encounters with the famous, infamous and fascinating, as well as the adrenalin-rush of beating a deadline, had, at the age of 40, lost their edge. Now the ever-critical, highly trained, caustic eye of the journalist was turning, relentlessly, in upon itself. It was the age-old question, that horny cliché, 'the meaning of life'.

Friendships undoubtedly eased the way. There were many – a rich source of pleasure, amusement, comfort, nourishment. But still. But still . . .

And then the telephone. The soft voice of an Australian Buddhist

1

nun, Yeshe Khadro, whom I'd known for a number of years both in England and on my travels to Nepal and India.

'Hello, Vicki. I have somebody who'd like a word with you.' The line went quiet and then through the telephone wires came a succession of gurglings, cooings and babblings that certainly seemed to make sense to the speaker.

Silence from my end. The other party, having got into his stride, was not to be stopped. He went on, and on.

'That,' said Yeshe Khadro when she finally got the receiver back, 'was Lama Osel'.

The silence this time was one of sheer amazement. Lama Osel was just 20 months old. A phenomenon I'd only heard about. For the past two months the Tibetan Buddhist circle of which I was a peripheral but sincere member had been buzzing with the extraordinary news of a Spanish child, the reincarnation of their much-loved, deeply respected Tibetan teacher, Lama Thubten Yeshe, who had died in California two and half years previously on 3 March 1984.

The depression suddenly vanished. I had known Lama Yeshe for eight years, had studied with him, laughed with him, and over that time developed a deep bond with him. More than any other person he had radically changed my life. I didn't realize how much until he'd died of a heart problem at the absurdly young age of 49. I mourned along with thousands of others whose lives he had touched. I still missed him greatly.

He had said, as a true Mahayana Buddhist, that when he died he would come back over and over again until he had helped lead all sentient beings to a state of Enlightenment. I'd listened and, because I knew he was not given to telling lies, had taken note. Reincarnation was an intriguing topic. I'd grappled with it until the idea of the continuity of consciousness manifesting in different physical forms made, at least, logical sense. We are all reborn ceaselessly – from 'beginningless time', I'd been told, but it is only the spiritual adept who can control the process and be reborn in a time and situation that best suits him to carry on his work.

That was the theory. Now I was being presented with the practice. Could it be true? Had Lama Yeshe actually kept his word and come back? Was it indeed possible to be reborn in the human body after you had died? And was it feasible to be able to dictate that process? These were monumental questions whose answers certainly delved beyond the superficial reaches of human existence.

This child was somebody I had to see. I hurriedly made an appointment to visit Lama Osel and his parents the next day during their brief stop-over in London. They were on their way to California to present Lama Osel to the people and place where he had passed away in his previous incarnation!

The next morning found me outside the door of London's Manjushri Centre, a nondescript semi-detached house in Finsbury Park, North London which Lama Yeshe had officially opened in 1978 to provide Tibetan Buddhist philosophy and meditation for world-weary souls in the great metropolis. It had a resident teacher, a large, round-faced, jolly, kind Tibetan called Geshe Wangchen (dispatched there by Lama Yeshe), a small band of dedicated helpers and a growing community of regular participants.

Yeshe Khadro, an attractive woman with the regulation cropped hair and maroon and gold robes, let me in.

There, standing behind her, in bright green dungarees was a solidly built toddler with short fair hair, chubby cheeks, high intelligent forehead and penetrating hazel eyes. He was absolutely absorbed in a toy – a ridiculous thing, a pair of eyes bouncing at the end of two springs attached to a headband and illuminated by a hand-controlled battery.

My mind, as well as my own eyes, gawped. How could this little child *possibly* be the great Tibetan teacher I had known so well? Lama Yeshe had brown skin, black hair, almond-shaped eyes, was 5 feet 7 inches tall, weighed 160 pounds, was in his 40s and was, well, Tibetan! How could I equate this fair-skinned, fair-haired, small western boy who could speak neither English nor Tibetan (nor Spanish for that matter) with our much-loved 'Lama', as everyone affectionately called him. Questions surged up. Does appearance, the outer show of feature and form that we come to associate with a certain name and personality, really constitute someone's true identity? What is a person anyway?

The child did not look up and say with a grin of recognition, 'Hello Vicki, good to see you again! How are you, dear? How's your family, dear?' (Lama called everyone 'dear'.) It was what I was half expecting. Lama Yeshe would have known me instantly.

Would have drawn me to him. Would have smiled, joked, emanated love, warmth, compassion – as he did with everyone.

This child hardly looked in my direction. No intimacy, no giggles. Nothing. He simply got on with his game. How *could* Osel be Lama Yeshe reborn? And yet the Lama's closest friend and colleague, Lama Zopa Rinpoche had conducted lengthy investigations and had verified that this child was indeed the reincarnation of Lama Yeshe.

The Dalai Lama himself, spiritual and temporal leader of the Tibetan people and a respected figure world-wide, had ratified Lama Zopa's findings, and publicly stated that Osel was indeed Lama Yeshe reborn. Neither of these eminent men were given to fabrication, and were certainly not in the business of creating sensations. They'd both stuck their necks out, and a lot was at stake. They must have been aware of the scepticism with which the West would greet their announcement.

And so in the first moments of that first meeting, my emotions a strange mixture of disappointment and still-lurking fascination, it seemed churlish if not arrogant to dismiss the judgement of these two spiritual masters out of hand. I decided to stay a little while, and watch. It seemed the least I could do.

As I looked at the stocky little green figure I began to smile. Completely detached from the curious stares focused upon him, he put the toy on his head. He walked up and down, flicking the switch to make the eyes shine. He stopped, then bounced his head up and down, watching the pattern the lights made on the carpet with some secret inner amusement. He toddled off into the garden, still having fun with his new plaything. There were no two ways about it. The little boy was an absolute clown. I roared with laughter. The mock solemnity with which he continued his private game only increased my mirth. He was undoubtedly sending himself up, finding delight in looking funny, and enjoying the absurdity of having an extra pair of eyes perched above his head.

And then it occurred to me. Wasn't Lama Yeshe always a one-man show? Lama Yeshe pulled faces, told jokes, had a wicked sense of mischief and sometimes engaged in the most outrageous antics if he thought they would get his message across. Most of all Lama Yeshe demonstrated beyond any possible doubt that to be holy did not mean being pompous, remote, cold, humourless.

I looked at Osel again. He seemed one of the most self-contained children I'd ever met. Certainly none of my friends' children of his age would play with a single toy with such concentrated attention for such a long period of time. He'd been at it for almost an hour now, with no signs of flagging. Nor was he at all affected by the covert stares of those gathered at the centre for the sole purpose of looking at him.

The next day I visited the Manjushri Centre again – this time to attend a special ceremony to welcome Osel to London. The meditation room was crowded with Lama Yeshe's former students who had come from all over England, anxious to see the living proof of reincarnation for themselves. No one knew what to expect, what to feel. As the chants and prayers began the door opened and Paco, Osel's father, entered carrying Osel in his arms, and placed him in the elevated seat (or 'throne' as it's called in the Tibetan tradition) usually reserved for teachers. None of us could quite believe our eyes. There before us was the littlest lama we'd ever seen. His green dungarees from yesterday had been exchanged for traditional Tibetan monks' clothing – a yellow undershirt and maroon robes. But in his hands he held his bottle and a toy ball. At his feet sat his former friend Geshe Wangchen and his parents, Paco Hita and Maria Torres.

Osel took us all in, then burst out laughing. It was glorious to hear. Although he looked entirely different physically, that peal of loud, spontaneous laughter could have come from Lama Yeshe himself. How often had he greeted us that way? It certainly broke the tension. In a few short minutes Osel was totally in command of the situation and was quickly generating the atmosphere of a picnic. This was no meek child being unnaturally coerced into a religious role (as I admit I'd half thought when I saw him wearing those robes and being put on the throne).

This child was a leader, an extrovert – one with an advanced sense of humour and a keen intelligence. A small child with enormous energy and charisma capable of capturing everyone's attention. I looked and looked. I didn't know what to think. Later I asked Geshe Wangchen what he believed. 'I have no absolute proof that Osel is Lama Yeshe, but somehow I feel, I feel here, that he is,' he said quietly, tapping his heart.

I went back to Paco and Maria and made an appointment to

visit them all in their home territory at Bubión in southern Spain. Ostensibly the journalist in me knew this was a story that would intrigue many, one that had to be followed up. Personally I had to see more of Osel and work out who or what he really was.

At home that evening, mulling over the strange events of the day, I suddenly remembered a dream I'd had a few months earlier. I was in a large room filled with a group of western Buddhists when Lama Yeshe walked in. He began talking and laughing with me and then went away. Shortly afterwards he reappeared with a baby, put it in my arms and walked off again. I was somewhat taken aback. It clearly wasn't my baby; in fact it belonged to one of the western followers, and I didn't know what he expected me to do with it. Lama Yeshe was obviously trying to show me something. And this was long before news of Osel reached me.

Could Osel be that Lama in a different form? A million uncertainties presented themselves. How would I ever know anyway? If Osel was already being put in robes, put on thrones and treated as Lama Yeshe, did he have a chance of being otherwise? He could, after all, be conditioned to fulfil a role. Hadn't the Jesuits always said, 'Give me a child until he's seven and he's mine for the rest of his life'? What was so different here? These were all questions I was fully determined to ask.

On the other hand it was perfectly logical that if Lama Yeshe had chosen to come back he would have chosen a western body. For Lama Yeshe's great work had been to bring his ancient, pure teachings to the West. As a Bodhisattva (one who forsakes Nirvana to return again and again to earth until all sentient beings are liberated) he would have been committed to the work he had started. And where better than among those he reached out to?

Lama Yeshe's overriding intention was to break down the barriers between peoples and to bridge the gap between East and West. He was a truly remarkable man, one of the most extraordinary I'd ever met.

1

THE MEETING

That my path crossed with Tibetan lamas at all can, in retrospect, only be regarded as fate – or 'karma', to use their language. Back in October 1976 it was the last thing on my mind. I was in my habitually frenetic office at the *Daily Mail* where I worked as a feature writer for the women's pages, when the telephone rang. It was Leslie Kenton, the health and beauty writer, wanting to speak to the editor. I'd met Leslie a year before, on a press trip to Switzerland, and we'd become friends. What was she up to?

'Actually, I'm going to Nepal to meditate with the lamas,' she replied. (Leslie always thoroughly researched any subject she was going to write about.) I heard myself say, 'How wonderful. What a superb thing to do.'

'Well, come with me,' suggested Leslie spontaneously.

'Why not? Yes, I will,' I heard the same voice reply.

She was leaving in three weeks' time.

It seemed a preposterous plan. I had not the slightest idea about Buddhism, lamas or Nepal. My knowledge of meditation was the same. Zero. It conjured up horrendous images of a lone figure left to face a blank wall for hours on end in a freezing courtyard until some inner gate opened to reveal ALL. (I'd obviously seen some third-rate movie about Zen masters sometime in my childhood.) I *knew* I'd never be able to do it. Introspection and sitting still were not for me. At best I'd last two days maximum. This meditation course was for a month.

Yet my astonishment at having agreed to such an extraordinary adventure was superseded by a strange conviction that what I was about to do was absolutely right. Having put the phone down I felt inexplicably happy. Very rarely have I had that strong sense that my life was 'right', that I'd got it 'on track' somehow, and all I had to do was let go and allow it to run where it should. Now was such a time.

Looking back, twelve years on, I can see I was absolutely ripe for the experience that was to follow. A long, difficult relationship had ended the previous year and I'd gone to Hong Kong seeking 'something' I sensed could only be found in the East. I didn't find it. My job as public relations consultant for the police (at the time when the chief of police was doing time for corruption) brought disillusionment and boredom. My flat was charming, looking out on to the South China Sea where the red-sailed junks moved silently in and out, but the people I met were primarily concerned with chasing the mighty dollar. After five months I crept back to London and the *Daily Mail*, crestfallen and depressed.

But the feeling that had prompted this disastrous escapade hadn't been entirely extinguished. I didn't realise it then, but it was a spiritual thirst, something that had been with me since childhood. I'd had a curious, but happily eclectic religious upbringing – my mother being Protestant and my father Roman Catholic. I'd been baptized Church of England, confirmed Anglo-Catholic, and taken in both Presbyterian schools and Catholic convents on my educational circuit of the world following my father, a Royal Naval Officer. We had slipped in and out of whatever church happened to be nearest to the place where we were living at the time. This broad-minded approach to religion pleased me (since even at that tender age I distrusted insular religious thought). Nowhere, however, could I find the answers to issues that nagged within. Jesus, I intuitively felt, had access to real wisdom that was never satisfactorily explained by the scriptures, church, nuns or priests. It wasn't enough to be told that He was the son of God. What made him able to walk on water and multiply the loaves and fishes? Since He was in human form I was sure it was more than those vague explanations 'Grace' and 'Faith' – and that His very humanity indicated that we had at least the potential to do likewise. He Himself had hinted at this several times: 'everything that I learned from my Father I have made known to you', and that most famous statement of all: 'The Kingdom of Heaven is within you'. I was yearning to know the 'hows' and the 'whys'.

Later, studying literature at university I caught glimpses of the Truth in the poems of William Blake and T. S. Eliot, but it was, like all poetry, elusive. I made a few forays into the western esoteric tradition, read books on spiritualism, visited mediums and found some inkling of an order that lay behind the outer appearance of things. The mysteries of the universe, the reasons why we are here, seen through the occult, are fascinating but ultimately did not satisfy me intellectually. The pronouncements of most mediums were not entirely to be trusted since their own imaginations often became intertwined with the material they were processing. How could you totally trust the pronouncements of disembodied spirits? (There are exceptions, like Rosemary Brown, who is world-renowned for the music she receives from 'dead' composers. I went to interview her for the *Daily Mail* in 1974. She subsequently became a close friend and over the years I have become well and truly convinced of the authenticity of her psychic powers, especially since they are based on a sincere Christian faith, and not on the spiritualist movement.)

What I think I was looking for was a living master. Someone I could see, touch, talk to. Someone who could tell me from their own experience the secrets, the wisdom I was yearning to hear. None of this was overt. I certainly never spoke of it to anyone, not even to myself. I hadn't actually formulated what I wanted in my own mind. It was just there, niggling away, and making me rather restless. And so I filled my days with the business of meeting deadlines and my nights with dinner parties, where the flow of what was considered to be witty conversation was generally outdone by the flow of wine. It was fun, fast, fashionable and frivolous.

In retrospect, it doesn't seem quite so strange that I agreed to go with Leslie to Nepal to meet the lamas. The frenzy of arranging air tickets, acquiring visas, vaccinations and thermal underwear – Nepal was cold in November and December – almost dispelled my anxiety about what I would find once I'd got there.

It wasn't at all as I'd expected. Kopan monastery, our destination, was built on a hill overlooking the Kathmandu Valley. It was beautiful. With its huge clumps of creaking bamboo, flowering frangipani trees, camellia bushes and prayer flags fluttering against a brilliant blue sky, and the Himalayan ranges in the background, the place seemed welcoming. The community was made up of a small group of Tibetan lamas, a mass of little boys in robes, being educated, and a handful of westerners who'd been ordained as Buddhist monks and nuns. They were all relaxed and smiling.

I was shown to my quarters – a small concrete room that I

was to share with seven other women of various ages, sizes and nationalities. On the floor were thin grass mats, where I rolled out my sleeping bag with some trepidation, and on the windows were bars which I rightly observed would do little to ward off the icy blasts coming off the Himalayas at night. It wasn't like home. No bathroom, no sink, no hot water (even the cold water had to be carried daily up the hill) and the loo was a hole in the ground.

The New York nun who showed us to our rooms recited the schedule. I paled. Up at 4.30 a.m. into the meditation tent by 5 a.m., soyabean coffee at 6 a.m., back to the tent for more meditation at 6.30 a.m., breakfast of porridge at 8 a.m., teachings at 9 a.m., more meditation at 11.30 a.m., lunch (vegetarian) at 12.30 p.m., discussion groups at 2 p.m., more teachings at 3.30 p.m., tea at 5.30 p.m., meditation at 6 p.m., hot chocolate at 7.30 p.m., more meditation at 8 p.m. Bed at 9 p.m.

This, I reckoned, totalled some 12 hours of sitting (cross-legged on a cushion) in the same place, next to the same people, every day for 30 days nonstop. Tibetans hold no truck with weekends and have no notion of a sabbath.

More followed. There was no alcohol, no tobacco, no drugs, no sex, no receiving or sending of mail, no radio, no newspapers, no books other than on related subjects (there was, of course, no TV or telephone in this remote spot) and no leaving the premises. These rules, I later learnt, were imposed to produce the most conducive environment to clear the mind for meditation, rather than with any punitive intent.

Two hundred of us from all over the world had heard the call to come to Kopan – drawn for our own very personal reasons. Most of the people were hippies, who'd made special detours from the hippy trail to meet the lamas. I eyed the 'freaks' as they called themselves, and they in turn eyed me. I'd never seen such a sea of Indian cotton in my life. They were agog at my cashmere jumper and Italian knit trousers – chosen strictly for warmth. After our initial mutual distaste we grew to like each other. I became particularly fond of the women in my room: Mo, a 22-year-old from Alaska, whose father was also in the navy and who'd been on the road for three years working on a fishing trawler and as a blue-movie film projectionist; Lynne, the Canadian, following gurus around India and photographing all the suffering she witnessed en route; gentle, brown-eyed Felicity from Australia, who was thinking of becoming a nun; and Suzanna, a gutsy Italian girl who was coming off heroin, having met Lama Yeshe. She had seen a lot of action – divorce, chronic depression, drug addiction and two attempted suicides. 'I know what it is like to feel dirty inside,' she said. Only when she met Lama Yeshe in France the previous year had she found a reason for living.

For all the apparent austerities, excitement was initially high. Here was high adventure indeed. The journalist in me saw precisely the potential of the 'story' I was living! Standing in silence on the hillside at dawn the next morning, watching the awe-inspiring orange sun rise over the white-capped peaks of the Himalayas, gradually revealing the swirling mists in the valley below with just the tips of the trees poking through, was an experience not given to many. Nor was being privy to the rites of Tibetan Buddhism, with its spine-chilling sound of massed reverberating mantra, the haunting sound of the long-horns and gongs, the strange multi-headed, multi-limbed deities depicted on bright wall-hangings throughout the meditation hall.

Rumours circulated about the lamas themselves. They were clairvoyant, had extraordinary psychic powers, didn't need sleep or food, some could fly, others could materialize and dematerialize their bodies at will. The very high ones, it was whispered, could 'die' in the lotus position, and remain like that for weeks on end, their bodies not decaying but sending forth sweet smells. It was all rich, mystical stuff.

The course was called 'Lam Rim', or 'The Graduated Path to Enlightenment.' No less. Brilliantly constructed by the 13th-century saint Tsong Ka Pa, founder of the largest school of Tibetan Buddhism, the Gelugpa sect, the Lam Rim plots in sequence the stages the spiritual aspirant should take on the journey to attain full liberation and union with the Ultimate. It was presented to us in long discourses by Lama Zopa Rinpoche, sitting on a high seat covered with bright brocade. Like some medieval sage, he carried his sacred text in a square of silk and lifted each loose page to read, book-binding never having reached Tibet.

Lama Zopa presented my first sight of a Tibetan spiritual master. He was the person we saw most on the course and the man who was to play such a crucial role in the drama that was to unfold.

My first impression I must admit, was not of a spiritual superman. He wore glasses and was small, thin and stooped from the tuberculosis he'd contracted in India, following his escape from Tibet after the Chinese invasion. But this bird-like, physically unprepossessing figure was somehow mysteriously transformed into a man of immense stature once aloft on his seat giving us the teachings of the Buddha. In his simple maroon and gold robes (red for compassion, gold for wisdom) he emanated a powerful mixture of absolute authority and total humility. He was utterly captivating. Here was authority without any trace of authoritarianism. Lama Zopa held us in his thrall. Prostrating three times before the image of the Buddha before and after he mounted the throne, he held forth tirelessly every day on the meaning of his ancient texts. He spoke as much from personal experience as from the scriptures. Never once in all that time did I see him lost for words, stumble over a meaning, hesitate, or get tired, irritable or angry. I'd never met a lecturer or priest like him. His sole wish was clearly to impart as much of his vast storehouse of knowledge as we could take. We flagged much quicker than he.

At first, gleaning his meaning was hard. Most of us couldn't understand a word he said. His poor pronunciation of English, punctuated by a constant cough, made listening to him an exasperating business. We'd come so far to learn the ancient wisdom and here it was, but it was still denied us. Strangely, after two or three days of persevering we all mysteriously 'tuned in' and got everything he said. We realized then what an eloquent speaker he was! And so he taught us the Lam Rim as extolled by the Buddha 2,500 years ago and passed on in an unbroken oral tradition to the man sitting before us.

He told us that this life was precious and should not be taken for granted, for it was rare and difficult to come by, and that the things we could achieve with it were vast. He spoke at length about death, its stark certainty and the grim uncertainty of its manner, time and place, to give us a heightened sense of living. He extolled the workings of karma, the universal law of cause and effect and how, because our every action of body, speech and mind creates a subsequent reaction, we are helplessly caught in the web of our own unconscious negativity and so circle endlessly on the wheel of birth and death without control. He talked about Mind or consciousness and how it functioned as a beginningless and endless stream, taking on new forms of material existence according to its propensities – the theory of Reincarnation. And he described in graphic detail the various 'states' that Mind can find – the stages of heaven and hell, which bore a remarkable similarity to Dante's versions, the Inferno and the Paradiso. This was the Buddha's diagnosis of the plight of the human condition; Lama Zopa went on to give us the cure. It was hard work. But I was struck by how clear and solid the doctrine was. Behind the words was the full force of centuries of a continuous tradition.

The way out of the whole sorry mess was to understand the profound wisdom of 'Emptiness' – the perennial philosophy that tells us first at an intellectual level and then at an intuitive one, that nothing in existence, including the concept of self, has any independent reality. When we stop grasping at all phenomena as if they were concrete and self-existent we become free. This was a thinking person's paradise. Here at last were the answers I'd been searching for. I recognized that the great gift and genius of Tibetan Buddhism was that it had formulated the path to the place which mystics of all religions had known. That place of indescribable bliss, of losing the ego and merging with the whole. Here at last the mysteries were made clear. When you break down the wall of false perception – our basic ignorance – everything is possible. The limits of Mind cease to exist; it is, as they said, beginningless and endless.

And then on top of that came the teachings on Compassion, the touchstone of Mahayana Buddhism which maintains that true liberation isn't possible unless you have a selfless heart. Long, long lessons teaching not just that we *must* love all sentient beings throughout all universes, but *how* to love them.

Lama Zopa talked about equanimity, the importance of balancing our feelings of liking, disliking and neutrality, and recognizing that it is always our ego that gets in the way and prevents us from feeling well-disposed towards everyone regardless of whether they please or displease us. On top of that we were told that every living creature is innately kind, and particularly kind to us, and without that kindness we would not be able to survive. Under Lama Zopa's tuition, even a cup of tea took on a completely new dimension when he enumerated all the creatures who had died in the planting and harvesting of the tea bushes and how many people had toiled in the sowing, picking, transporting, packaging and marketing. With the Tibetans the preciousness of life is sanctified everywhere. The kindness of others, especially your mother who gave you life, must be repaid. How far from the modern psycho-analytical approach which points the finger of blame at parents and early childhood for all one's woes.

To the lamas the attainment of the highest wisdom, Emptiness, was not enough. Emptiness, they said, led to Nirvana, the cessation of suffering, but that was a hollow victory when all around were stuck in the mire of their own self-inflicted but unknowing misery. Nirvana, was still, ultimately, an ego-trip. And so those following the Tibetan Buddhist way pledged themselves to forsake the bliss of Nirvana in order to return again and again to all levels of suffering existence until they had shown each and every sentient being the way out. It was a longer, more arduous path, but the only way to true enlightenment. A being who had made such a promise was called 'Bodhisattva' or, 'Noble One'.

It was all handed to us on a plate – first through Lama Zopa's discourses and then in meditation. Much to my amazement, I discovered I could, after a fashion, meditate. Here was no system of facing a blank wall for hours on end or reciting a secret mantra to attain transcendental bliss; we were taught instead to still or quieten the mind through focusing our attention on the coming and going of the breath and then to direct our concentration on to the subject of the teachings. We were led through the meditation by a monk who gave us the salient points of the discourse we had just listened to. The idea was to contemplate them and relate them to our own experiences. In this way the path to enlightenment was transferred to the heart from the head and thus became real. Only when this had happened could the transformation begin.

Still, it wasn't easy. As I began to meditate it instantly became clear how totally out of control my mind was, dashing hither and thither in the hectic pursuit of a million irrelevant, disconnected, trivial thoughts. And all those aspects of myself usually buried beneath the busyness and distractions of my normal everyday life began to surface: irritability, anger, frustration, jealousy, doubt, fear, insecurity, pride – the whole distasteful gamut. For the first time in my life I not only had to confront them, but take responsibility for them – the Buddha's First Noble Truth being that you must first recognize your own suffering before you can eliminate it. We might have been sitting still in the midst of the mighty Himalayas but we were scaling the mountains of the mind, a far more daunting task. The words of Carl Jung had never seemed so apt: 'Space flights are merely an escape, a fleeing away from oneself; because it is easier to go to Mars or the Moon than it is to penetrate one's own being.'

And so I grappled with aching knees, tough physical conditions, the teachings and meditations and in doing so found I went far beyond the 'journalistic' interest that ostensibly prompted me in the beginning. I was getting a glimpse of what Thomas Merton, the Trappist author-priest who studied eastern religions, rightly described as the most complex and comprehensive spiritual system known to men.

Not that I agreed with it all. There was much that was alien, not just the cultural presentation but the content as well. Thankfully, we were allowed to dissent. Lamas, I learnt, liked nothing better than a good argument. Indeed they were skilled debaters and threw themselves heartily into any discussion on the Dharma (as the spiritual path was generally called). The Way of Tibetan Buddhism is through personal exploration and individual testimony of the truth. The Buddha himself said: 'The learned ones treat my teachings like gold. They test it, by rubbing it, cutting it and burning it. Likewise my teachings. Do not have blind faith.' It suited my naturally questioning, sceptical mind well.

I had serious misgivings however, as to the suitability of the teachings for the West in general. They were psychologically, philosophically and spiritually brilliant but the strong cultural overtones and the severe medieval context made them, I reckoned, virtually impossible for 20th-century western man to assimilate. Lama Zopa was giving us the teachings straight down the line, just as they had been delivered by Tsong Ka Pa in 13th-century Tibet. It was hard to swallow. The talk of hell, the retribution of karma, the belief in various types of ghosts and gods, deities that looked like blue bulls, others that had a thousand arms, and several heads. I couldn't see it being accepted in Clapham! It was a shame. In essence it had so much to offer.

At the peak of my exasperation and despair at this outmoded

delivery, in walked Lama Yeshe. He wended his way between us, round, jolly, beaming happiness and saying unaccountably as he went, 'Thank you', 'Thank you so much', 'Thank you'. (It was only later that I learnt that the highest level of spirituality is characterized by a state of gratitude.) Lama Yeshe thanked everyone all the time, whether they were sunbathing on the grass outside his room or listening to four hours of his teaching.

His impact on me was immediate. I had never seen such warmth, such an abundance of joy, such an overwhelming humanity in anyone. Lama Yeshe dispelled in one moment any notion I had that an eastern sage was cold and inscrutable, having transcended trivial things like emotion and feeling ages ago. Having done his prostrations before the Buddha and climbed up on to his seat, he took one look at us all and burst out laughing.

'Any problems?' he enquired, and roared with laughter again. He must have known, somehow, the myriad questions that were going through our minds at that stage. Someone dared to ask it: How could Tibetan Buddhism be integrated into a normal everyday western life?

'Each must do according to his or her own level,' he replied and then launched into the most incongruous English I'd ever heard, gleaned from the hippies, his first encounter with the West. 'Buddhism, meditation, is not blissing out. It's not some kind of trip. You do not think "I am so special . . . I am doing some special kind of eastern meditation",' he continued, giving a hilarious pantomime of a westerner filled with self-importance, trying to meditate. 'Buddhism is an inner thing. It is seeing and growing your own potential. Everyone has Buddha-nature, has his or her own wisdom and compassion.

'Don't get hung up on all these oriental forms. A Buddha just means a Fully Awakened Being. That's all. He doesn't have to have yellow skin and slanting eyes. Every culture Buddhism has gone into has painted the Buddha in its own way. The West will create western Buddhas. It doesn't matter,' he said.

The exasperation and despair vanished. Here was a lama speaking my language (or my language of a sort!). Gone were the medieval words from the medieval texts. Here was modern psychological man but with shaved head, robes and emanating that special quality that was the indefinable but irrefutable spiritual truth.

Lama Yeshe continued to talk directly to us, answering our questions and giving us his explanation of Mahayana Buddhism. Together with the purist line delivered by Lama Zopa it made, finally, the complete picture. They were the perfect couple. One introvert, one extrovert; one conventional, one not. Two sides of the same coin. But it was Lama Yeshe who reached out to me. I'd never seen anyone make so much effort to communicate. He used his entire body to get his message across, pulling faces, waving his arms, teasing, even aping us. He came out with the most outrageous statements: 'The Dharma is like an American bed – everyone can fit in! You clever people, you think your supermarket enjoyment is real, but I'm telling you you're so miserable. However, you can transform this miserable into everlasting blissful chocolate! Ha! Now you going to say "he crazy, he Himalayan gorilla!" Well, I'm saying, you just check up.'

In spite of his scrambled English we all understood precisely what he was saying. Our supermarket world with its overabundance of material goods was not alleviating the mental unrest and disease that lay buried not too deep beneath the surface. Lama had delivered his message with a verve and dynamism that was irresistible. If I wasn't exactly buying all of Tibetan Buddhism I certainly bought him. He was all that I had imagined a spiritual master should be: radiant, filled with a zest for life, yet at the same time an acute sensitivity for our innate sorrow; unerringly wise; suffused with humility; completely ego-less; and overflowing with an irrepressible sense of humour. Struck by life's absurdity, a joke, or spontaneous joy, he would burst forth into peals of laughter, rocking back and forth on his throne, throwing his robes over his head, hitting himself with his rosary. If this was holiness, it was worth emulating.

I later made an appointment to see him. I wanted to get a closer look, to see if the Lama Yeshe effect was the same on an individual as on an audience. With some trepidation I climbed the stairs to his tiny room at the top of the Gompa, removed my shoes and went in.

He was sitting on a low seat covered with a Tibetan carpet and indicated that I should sit on the cushion by his side. I don't remember much of that conversation (I had no burning issue to discuss) except that he made me feel instantly relaxed, as if I had known him for years. I could have chatted to him about anything. His warmth and humanity were enormous. At one stage he leant across and said, 'You and me, dear, we have good communication.' At the time I thought he was just pointing out the obvious – that we could talk. Later, this seemingly trivial remark was to take on added significance.

I descended the stairs feeling uplifted and strangely happy. I didn't know it then but Lama Yeshe had touched something in me, and I would never be quite the same again. When I left him and Kopan a few days later, I genuinely thought I'd never see either of them again. There seemed no reason to – which just indicates how little wisdom I had.

Leslie Kenton and I flew out of Nepal as abruptly as we had flown in. Our friendship had been sealed by that unique shared experience. Leslie's homecoming heralded the start of her hugely successful career as an author – her first book, *The Joy of Beauty*, was inspired by the insights she had acquired from her time with the lamas. For me the culture shock of my re-entry into London was to prove far greater than the shock of the austerities I'd encountered on that first fateful step into the Tibetan Buddhist monastery.

2

THE WEST IS THE TEST

Against the backdrop of my familiar surroundings and old friends, the meaning of that month in Kopan finally hit me. I had changed. The roar of the great metropolis that formerly filled me with excitement I found unbearable; the dinner parties bored and exhausted me; the conversation I once thought witty now seemed trivial and a sad cover-up for a life that was fundamentally lacking in meaning; I wanted to go to bed at 9 o'clock. Most of all it was the faces that I saw on the street and in the tube which so distressed me. They were marked with a slow tension and heaviness, the penalty for keeping up with the frenetic pace of western society, in return for the 'rewards' of a bigger car and four weeks' holiday abroad. Was this the most we could get out of our 'precious human life'? Was this the most we could do with our vast human potential? I was, involuntarily, 'checking up', as Lama Yeshe had admonished us.

More radically, my career took an immediate U-turn. In all conscience I could no longer continue to meet the demands of fast, full-time, tabloid journalism, with its emphasis on impact rather than truth. How could I die a happy death knowing I'd lived out most of my professional life engaged in trivia, warping the facts more often than not, and hurting many people along the way? I decided to go freelance so that I could have more control over what I wrote. It was to prove nervewracking at the beginning, and always financially precarious, though ultimately the professional and personal satisfaction more than compensated.

But Kopan and the lamas had given me much more. In those first few weeks following my return I experienced a peace and inner happiness I had never thought possible. The pay-off from all those arduous hours sitting with aching knees in the cold and sometimes dark, meditating. Who could have guessed it would give so much? The inner life was stirring. Now I knew that whatever life presented, it was my mind's reaction to it that caused the pain or the happiness. The responsibility was mine, but so was the control. For hadn't I also been told during those 30 days of non-stop Buddhist tuition that everything in life is perpetually changing (to expect otherwise is to court suffering)? And the only true source of security lies within.

In spite of the madness of the life going on around me I realized I had found something that was truly sane. Just before Christmas I switched on the radio and heard a programme about that great 14th-century British mystic, Mother Julian of Norwich. Her final vision of optimism, having relived through a series of visions Christ's agony on the cross, perfectly echoed what I was feeling: 'All shall be well, and all shall be well, and all manner of things shall be well.'

I meditated every morning, this time propped up on my pillows on my inner sprung mattress, trying to keep alive the small flame which had been ignited within. Inevitably the Kopan effect wore off after a few months, and so did the meditations. That they had lasted so long can, in retrospect, only be attributed to the power of the genuine article. But the strain of living within that fast-moving materialistic world, combined with the mental habits accumulated over a lifetime, eroded the peace and tranquillity I had so unexpectedly found. That autumn, with chronic back pain caused through nervous tension, it dawned on me that I was actually missing the serenity I'd brought back with me from Nepal. It had ebbed away so gradually I hadn't noticed it going. If I'd had it once maybe I could get it again. This time I headed not for the Orient but to the far more accessible Manjushri Institute, an awesome Victorian Gothic mansion on the shores of Morecambe Bay in Ulverston, Cumbria, recently founded by Lama Yeshe's students in Britain.

It was to be the start of a still-continuing pattern of trying to integrate Tibetan Buddhist philosophy into a normal everyday western lifestyle. Not for me did the maroon and gold robes ever beckon. I had no wish to shave my head and become Tibetan in any way. Nor could I happily embrace the rich trappings of Buddhist ritual, which had no apparent relevance to anything within my own cultural heritage. No. For me, if Buddhist teachings were to have any real value they had to be applicable to the world I came from. The West was the test.

And so over the following years I bounced back and forth — from my London existence to various Tibetan Buddhist centres, 'checking up'. There continued to be aspects of the doctrine I couldn't accept (I was never an easy believer) but Tibetan Buddhism in general and Lama Yeshe in particular were potent enough forces to keep me vitally interested, and still questioning.

When Lama Yeshe came to England to give a course at Manjushri Institute one summer I hurried up there. There were a lot of things on my mind. The most burning issue, however, was God. Buddhists don't believe in a Creator, a single primary cause for existence. They maintain that such a premise is both illogical and impossible since a primary cause *has* to have a preceding cause. They talk instead of 'beginningless and endless Mind'. This worried me. My Christian background was too strong to be eradicated by a couple of short Buddhist meditation courses. What made the trees grow if it wasn't the creative force called God? What was the mastermind principle behind everything if not God?

Lama Yeshe looked exactly the same as at Kopan, emanating goodness, goodwill, humour, humility and that indefinable quality which can only ineptly be described as inner wisdom. He'd conducted the course with his unique charisma. As before, I sat enthralled. I realized it wasn't so much the words alone that conveyed the meaning, but his very being. We could see, and hear, and sense what he was getting at — which in Buddhist teachings always boils down to the same thing, the Awakened Being — because we had one sitting before us. Or at least someone who was as close as we were going to get to an Awakened Being.

I saw my chance of tackling Lama about the God issue one afternoon when we were all enjoying a picnic lunch on the lawns outside. He let me struggle through the tortured intricacies of my question, beamed, and abruptly turned the question back on me. 'What do *you* think God is? Is He an old man in the sky?', he asked. 'Well, no. Of course not. He is a principle, a creative force, a law of love,' I feebly replied, realizing with embarrassment what woolly notions I actually had about God. Lama looked me straight in the eye: 'God is Mind, Buddha is Mind — both are totally open omniscient Mind. They are the same thing,' he said.

Not totally convinced I went away and 'checked up' some more. I found a Christian priest who'd attended Lama's course walking in full robes down by the sea-shore. How could he of all people equate Christian doctrine with a Tibetan Buddhist course? Didn't it confuse him?

'At the very fundamental level, we have a lot in common. There are many similar aspects, particularly the altruistic motivation, the doctrine of loving your neighbour and turning the other cheek,' he said. 'On the next level we part company – Buddhism has no theory of God for instance. But at the top level we meet again and there is no separation. We speak the same language, but without words.' I nodded, sensing rather than knowing what he meant. The Truth must be the Truth no matter by which path you approach it.

A Zen story I had once heard came to mind. A large Buddhist college in Japan decided they should do something positive to help bridge the gap between all the major religions of the world. They duly organized a conference and invited all the leading authorities of the principal faiths, who sat around a large table enjoying lively debate and philosophical exchange. After they had all gone home the Zen masters then decided they should repeat the exercise but this time inviting the highest spiritual practitioners of the main religions. This time there was no talking, no debate – the masters merely sat round the big table smiling at each other and nodding their heads.

Still mulling over 'God', although by this time the Buddhist explanation was intellectually, if not emotionally, far more satisfying, I came across a transcript of a talk Lama Yeshe had given in Italy on 'Mind and Mental Factors'. It not only gave insights into the extreme depth and profundity of Lama Yeshe's wisdom but more clues about God.

'Now there are two things,' he said. 'One is existent reality – the existent reality of the object world. The second is the comprehension – the concepts of consciousness, which understands what exists. In Tibetan we call it Yul – object – and Yul-chen – consciousness. And the Tibetan explanation is such: Reality and consciousness embrace each other. They are completely one.

'Now Christians describe God in terms of being omnipresent, don't they? God is omnipresent, He completely embraces reality, totally. It is said like this.

'And in Buddhism it says, consciousness is omnipresent, it

completely embraces all existence, externally and internally, under the earth and in the sky, whatever there is. So there is no existence which cannot be comprehended by consciousness. This concept, this theory seems simple. But I'm sure for many western minds it's not simple. Check up. Check up!'

It was certainly something to chew over.

My next meeting with Lama Yeshe was in Dharamsala, in northern India, home of the Dalai Lama and the Tibetan government-in-exile. Lama had issued personal invitations to various students around the world urging them to come to Dharamsala where His Holiness was giving tantric teachings on the 'Mahamudra' for the first time to westerners in his own temple. I didn't get an invitation but decided to join two friends who were going. On arriving at the only hotel in this beautiful hilltop station (once patronized by the ladies of the Raj during the Indian summer months) I immediately bumped into Lama. I said I hoped he didn't mind my coming since I hadn't been invited. 'Oh no, dear. You and I have special communication.' There it was again. What did it mean? He said no more, making polite small talk, and went on his way.

During the 10-day course, where we sat inside the temple at the feet of the remarkable Dalai Lama, and the venerable Tibetan lamas sat outside listening to the teachings through loudspeakers, Lama Yeshe took special care of his western flock. We were on show. So many westerners had come to Tibetan Buddhism through him and he was clearly looking after us. During the week he took a group of us up the steep mountain path to his retreat centre, a beautiful old colonial house complete with verandah and spectacular views of Himachal Pradesh below. It had been snowing heavily during the week – the biggest snowflakes I had ever seen – and as we paused en route to catch our breath a large clump of snow fell from an overhead branch and went straight down the back of my jacket. Lama saw and burst out laughing. 'That's God blessing you!' he joked. He clearly hadn't forgotten the conversation we'd had at least two years before. He then posed happily for a photograph next to a large snowman someone had made. I knew then that he knew my mind completely. Surprisingly I didn't mind at all.

Our next encounter was back in London where I'd been helping to organize his visit which included a public talk in St John's, Smith Square. My duty was to ferry Lama about in my car – a modest Ford polished and washed for the first time in months for the occasion. It was the first time I'd had the opportunity to be really informal with Lama over any length of time. Driving about London together, with him in the front seat next to me, he asked all sorts of personal questions.

'Was I married?' 'No.' 'Had I ever wanted to be?' 'Not really – the domestic life had never really appealed.' 'Had I ever wanted children?' 'Never.' Lama nodded his approval. 'You do not need those things. They can also bring much suffering,' he said, voicing my own sentiments exactly. The approval from such a wise being was reassuring. The bond between us was deepening.

On the last day of his visit he gave teachings to a small gathering at the October Gallery in Old Gloucester Street, and at the end everyone lined up to receive his blessing. I noticed each person was carrying a small gift – except me. I hung back until the very end, embarrassed at my thoughtlessness. When, finally, my turn came I said hastily, 'Lama, I'm afraid I have nothing to give you.' He leant down and, with his face almost touching mine, replied in a whisper charged with meaning, 'I only want your heart.' I was speechless. To give the heart, the ultimate surrender, was the hardest thing of all, but the only gift worth giving.

For all this I never thought of Lama as a 'guru' in the sense that the word has come to be used by most westerners – a character to whom you totally dedicate your life, forsaking any autonomy of thought or action. This was a position that Lama Yeshe never courted and I certainly would never accept. In fact he was always totally unimpressed by the 'guru business' that some students tried to inflict on him, preferring people to act naturally and be themselves at all times. He hated obsequiousness of any kind.

He once said, 'I would have hated it if my teacher had told me "drink this", "eat this". I prefer to use my own intelligence, my own intuition, make my own decisions. Similarly, you should all make your own lives, trusting your own Buddha-nature. Of course listen to advice, but ultimately, trust your own intelligence.'

With my own fiercely independent nature it was the only stand I could ever agree with. Later, reading *The Way of the White Clouds*, by Lama Govinda, I got a truer picture of the real function of a guru: 'A guru is far more than a teacher in the ordinary sense. A teacher gives knowledge but a guru gives himself. The real teachings of a guru are not his words but what remains unspoken, because it goes beyond the power of human speech. The guru is an *inspirer*, in the truest sense of this word, i.e. one who infuses us with his own living spirit.'

In this light I was more than willing to accept Lama Yeshe as my guru.

3

LAMA – THE MAN

Over the years many fascinating and amusing stories reached me about Lama Yeshe which helped build a more complete picture of the man, and which convinced me further that he was, indeed, an extraordinary being. Nothing, it seemed, was too outrageous or outlandish for him to try if it meant getting a clearer insight into the society his disciples came from, the influences that had helped shape their minds. Coming from an extremely conventional background himself, his broadmindedness was revolutionary. He was a big man. His principal aim in life was to reach out to all people, traversing geographical, racial and philosophical boundaries with the universality of his message.

In Hong Kong, for instance, he had taken off his robes, put on trousers, shirt and tie and taken himself off to the night-club in his hotel, curious to see for himself what westerners considered sophisticated entertainment. Who knows what he really thought. He was always telling people to have a good time, but thereafter whenever he wanted to use a derisory term to sum up people wasting time he called them 'night-clubbers'.

In Australia he donned shorts, a T-shirt and a broad-brimmed hat and went 'walkabout' for a week. No one knew where he had disappeared to. On his return, sporting a fine sun-tan he announced he'd been visiting beaches, since this was obviously the Australian version of a 'good time'.

Likewise, on a trip to America, he astonished not a few by playing the tables at Las Vegas! He then dragged a reluctant Lama Zopa (who by inclination would much prefer meditating in his room), not only to Disneyland, where he tried most of the rides and wore a Mickey Mouse hat – but also to a strip joint, where they both sat eating ice-cream, not at all shocked by the antics of the lady on the stage. Lama was certainly never a prude. Not only did he come from a society where all bodily functions, including sex, were accepted without the neurotic overtones our more 'civilized' world has endowed them with, but as a Lama he had made a detailed study of sexual energy, learning how to utilize it on the spiritual path. As a result, westerners found he was surprisingly good at listening to sexual problems, and giving precise, excellent advice.

His worldly education took another quantum leap when, after talking to a gay disciple in San Francisco, he asked to be taken to a gay bar and later to the Gay Parade. He enjoyed himself enormously and, by all reports, asked endless questions. He was understandably fascinated by the gay scene, such a phenomenon not having reached Tibet, and wanted to know in very intimate detail, how it started, what the gays wanted, and what they did! There was never any hint of disgust or disapproval, merely a thirst for knowledge. His verdict at the end of his unusual day out was that in his opinion the male gays were better-looking than the females! Lama was like an anthropologist, turning the tables and studying us. Seeing what kind of species we were, what strange eating, drinking, social and mating habits we had. Were we really the backward, barbaric people his countrymen generally believed us to be?

His behaviour on these field trips and his general intimacy with his western students, including women, caused quite a few raised eyebrows among his more conservative fellow lamas and the Tibetan community at large – although the Dalai Lama and several high-ranking lamas in the spiritual hierarchy understood entirely the nature of the mission he had embarked on. But those with narrower vision felt that he was in some way violating his vows. Lama Yeshe himself told the story of how his sister who lived in Delhi came to him one day with tears in her eyes, begging him to leave the westerners and let her support him financially to go on a long retreat and resume the path he had abandoned. On another occasion, again with some members of his family in Dharamsala and one or two western students, he began to speak of the return trip he had made to Tibet the previous month. He told, in a grim voice, of a priceless Buddha statue the Chinese had thrown into the bottom of a river. He told it again and began to laugh. The laughter increased in volume, 'The Buddha-statue was in ruins in the river,' he roared. The brothers and sisters looked on aghast at such irreverence. Had Lama Yeshe lost his mind? Only the westerners present understood his meaning. It didn't matter if the Buddha statue was in ruins since it is the internalized meaning of the Buddha's message and not the outward form that is to be venerated.

For all his compassion he was never timid about driving his meaning home. 'Dharma should not be comfortable. It should shake! We are not in the business of being polite,' he would say, as he delivered some devastating psychological or spiritual truth about us.

He was right. We learnt that way. Not that he ever hurt us. Lama managed to lay bare our foolish ways, our delusions, with infinite compassion and with the overriding confidence that ultimately good would conquer all. And having delivered some home truth he'd laugh, and we'd all laugh with him, comforted that in spite of our faults, this man would be with us all the way to liberation. And although he was unfailingly polite in his manners, a true gentleman, he was never soft with those who tried to cheat him. He had been known to grab Indian railway porters by the scruff of their necks and shake them when they'd tried to steal something. I always liked these 'tough' stories about Lama Yeshe because they proved that to be a spiritual being you did not have to become a wimp.

In fact as he became more familiar with the West, Lama Yeshe began to take an active interest in politics. Wherever he was, the first thing he'd do was switch on the TV and watch the adverts because they told him about the psychology of that country. He also watched the news, and would have political magazines read to him from cover to cover. He began to formulate strong political opinions which confirmed that he was no 'wet'.

One day, in California, he saw a television programme about the new souped-up version of the B52 bomber – black, menacing, nasty – with a man standing beside it, absolutely dwarfed. He was fascinated. He asked further questions about what it could do. This was at the time when Iran had captured the American hostages and Lama Yeshe was appalled by this and President Carter's weak stance. 'President Carter talks all the time about human rights but it's just words. I don't respect him,' announced Lama. He then declared what he would do in Jimmy Carter's position: 'I would take a couple of hundred B52 bombers and fly them to Tehran, but first telling the Soviet Union I was not going to bomb. I would have these big planes fly wing to wing, like a big black cloud, right over Tehran, so low that the noise would terrify everyone and break every window in every building. And then I would drop pamphlets saying that if we have to sacrifice 52 lives it will make us very angry and we will come back and there will be no more Tehran – unless the hostages are given back within 48 hours with not one single hair on their head harmed.' Lama clearly wasn't on a love and peace trip. He was an intensely practical man, and a born leader.

His originality found perhaps its greatest expression in his altar. He always stressed that an altar should be a personal affair, endowed with items that had special meaning for each individual. On *his* altar he placed a toy aeroplane, saying that this was the hallowed means whereby he could reach his students and spread the Buddha's teachings. It wasn't conventional, but Lama could see no point in hanging on to the trappings of Tibetan-style Buddhism, if he found something better to replace it with from the West. For instance he unceremoniously did away with his traditional incense, replacing it instead with spray perfume, which he much preferred and found easier to use! 'We must develop western-style Buddhism,' he would say.

His travels brought him into contact with more than just the rich material trappings of western life, it showed him Christianity in its living form. Lama Yeshe, being naturally broadminded, was a true ecumenicist. Long before he came to the West he'd developed a deep and sincere respect for Jesus Christ. Indeed one Christmas he had given the most profound teachings on the meaning of that event and how we should prepare ourselves for it (later to be published as *Silent Mind Holy Mind*). Now he had the opportunity to examine it at source. One day while in Pisa he rushed up to Lama Zopa, took him by the hand, and said with undisguised excitement, 'Come, I have something to show you. I have found something wonderful.' He led Lama Zopa to Assisi where he triumphantly showed him St Francis's cave. 'There, you see there are yogis in the West, who also use caves,' he said. Lama Zopa later provided the pointed addendum that although St Francis might have reached enlightenment he didn't leave any books telling anyone else how to do it!

Whenever he could Lama would visit Christian monasteries and talk to the monks there. He was always impressed with what he found. 'We Buddhists *talk* a lot about Bodhicitta [compassion], a lot of blah, blah, blah, but the Christians go and do it,' he said on one occasion. And on another: 'You say Christians have no meditations, but that's wrong conception! I tell you, that's wrong,' he said emphatically.

When he died, a French Roman Catholic priest, Father P. Bernard de Give, who had met Lama Yeshe in Provence in 1978 when he attended a 10-day retreat, wrote the most glowing tribute which revealed that Lama had indeed known how to go beyond the traditional confines that so often separate the great religions: 'So he has left us, this marvellous being who was all smiles, who simply breathed goodness. I believe I express the feeling of all those who knew him when I confess I must hold back tears when I think that never again will I see that radiant face, filled both with a joy for life and awareness of suffering that affects the inner soul of all human beings ... Please permit this Christian monk to recall a few memories of one who was for many both a master and a friend ...

'Of Lama Yeshe one could only say that he had his audience in his pocket. He triumphed with his good satire of western society. He was an incomparable stage artist, one might almost say a clown of frequently comic mimicry. And though he succeeded in laying bare the oddities and foolish ways, the delusions of the masses dominated by their passions, never did he hurt anyone. Rather one felt touched by his unbelievable compassion and utter confidence in the inevitable victory of good. And when he gave himself up to fits of laughter, everyone would follow him, as though convinced that with this man by their side they were heading towards liberation.'

Part of Lama's universal appeal was his enormous vitality, the boundless energy with which he infused every gesture, word and look. He oozed life. (How were we to know that all the time he was desperately ill?) This enthusiasm spilled into his hobbies. He had a passion, amongst other things for driving – not shared incidentally by anyone who had to travel with him. Having got his licence in California, he took to the wheel with a flair that was literally nerve-racking. Although he never had an accident, he would miss everything on the road, moving or stationary, by inches. It was a test of guru devotion to sit next to him. One day, careering down the highway in New Zealand, he looked in his rear mirror and saw to his dismay a traffic cop on a motor bike roaring up behind him, lights flashing, siren sounding. He waved Lama down. Not only had he been speeding, he'd been travelling without his lights on. As the traffic offence was duly written in the book, Lama astonished the policeman by saying over and over again, 'Thank you, Thank you so much, Thank you – so kind!'

He was also an avid gardener and a keen cook. In his later years he became quite a connoisseur of health food, swapping his traditional tsampa and tugpa (roasted ground barley flour made into dumplings, and noodle vegetable stew) for crunchy wholegrain bread, fresh green salads and herb teas. He travelled everywhere with 'Earl Grey'. He loved food and would often take to the kitchen, concocting delicious dishes which he'd serve to all present – leaving someone else to clean up the mess he'd left behind. This love of food was to have an unusual pay-off one day. An Italian woman, staying at Kopan, decided to go into Kathmandu where, feeling slightly bored, she came across a newly arrived group of Italian tourists, who she invited 'to meet a genuine Tibetan lama'.

This was in the early Kopan days when Lama Yeshe was usually accessible to whoever wanted to see him. Arriving back at Kopan, with all her tourists in tow, the Italian woman saw Lama Yeshe and explained she'd invited them all to tea. 'Well, you go ahead, make the tea,' said Lama, making no move toward the group. He could tell they had no spiritual interest and was not prepared to be displayed as a token lama. Embarrassed now, the woman asked if he couldn't join them for a little while. Lama replied that he might come for an hour (a very short time in Lama Yeshe's book).

He did come, sat down among the group and politely asked the man next to him where he'd come from. 'Milan,' replied the tourist. 'Ahh,' said Lama, his whole face lighting up, 'Risotto Milanese! So *good*.' The man, rather taken aback that a Lama should know of the culinary jewel in Milan's crown, sat up. Lama went on to reel off the best way to make Risotto Milanese. The Italian was ecstatic. Lama was getting into his stride. 'And you know that little restaurant behind the Duomo, *that* is the best place for risotto in Milan.' The man was speechless with admiration. 'And you,' continued Lama, smiling at a woman in the group, 'where are you from?' 'Roma,' replied the woman. 'Roma has the most wonderful spaghetti carbonara,' enthused Lama, and continued to expound the methods for making it, the best pepper to use, the right kind of cheese.

The Italian woman who'd invited the group couldn't believe her ears. Lama had only been to Italy once, for a whistle-stop 10-day tour. She had no idea how he could have picked up such detailed information about Italian cuisine. Lama carried on in this vein with the entire group, exhibiting profound knowledge of their regional dishes. They were utterly captivated, for to the Italian a man can be a brain surgeon but without appreciation of food he remains an ignoramus. Lama was clearly a man worthy of respect. Fifty-five minutes had gone by. Lama then dropped into one of his profound silences. For two minutes no one said anything. Then, out of the silence, the first man spoke: 'Is it true that there is such a thing as Enlightenment?' The flood gates had broken. A torrent of questions about man's spiritual potential, Tibet, Buddhism followed. With supreme timing Lama looked at his watch. 'I'm sorry,' he said, 'I have no more time now. But if you want to know more about these things I am coming to Italy next year. You can get the information from the woman over there.' As a communicator, he was unsurpassable.

Lama had an advantage in this respect. He could read people's minds. Not that he ever flaunted this (no lama would ever advertise his power, rightly believing it would be a hindrance to the follower's spiritual progress) but one gathered it over days of being with him. So many of us on the Kopan course would find snippets of conversation we'd had with each other being repeated by Lama, especially if they had some relevance to the topic being discussed. It was uncanny. He could also pick up on things we'd been doing – supposedly in private. The lamas could even enter our dream states. A friend of mine learnt this way that she was pregnant – a fact she ratified on her immediate return to London. But most of all we discovered that our questions, especially those unvoiced, would be answered within the next discourse. We'd all go into the lecture tent with our heads full of some problem or another (often highly personal) and we'd find within the talking the answer we were seeking. It wasn't vague, it was explicit and undeniably directed at the individual, although couched in language that would cause no embarrassment, nor give any clue as to the questioner's identity.

One boy thought he'd test out Lama's psychic power by seeing if he would tune in to a deliberate thought directed at him. During the next discourse he visualized a large, cold glass of freshly squeezed orange juice and proceeded to offer it to him. Lama stopped what he was saying, looked at the boy, said 'Thank you dear, very nice,' and got on with the discourse.

All this, so subtly done, gave an intimation of the vast minds of the beings who were teaching us. They were obviously capable of reading several minds simultaneously, while being outwardly occupied with something else. They were living examples of the vast potential of human consciousness, which they told us was everybody's birthright. The lamas grew in stature before our very eyes. They were supermen! And yet never for one second did they lose their outer aspect of humility, humanity and humour. Who exactly were they?

4

THE BEGINNING

The world that Lama Yeshe came from could not have been further from the one he was to find himself in. To travel to Tibet even now is to go back in time five centuries or more. This is what the Middle Ages in Europe must have looked like. It is a country that has been held in a time warp, its way of life, customs, belief systems and spirituality literally kept on ice in splendid isolation on the roof-top of the world.

Lama Yeshe was born in a small, mountainous village called Tolung, not far from Lhasa, in May 1935. His parents were farmers, and for them, like most Tibetans, life was hard, poor and stripped to the bare necessities. Nevertheless it was a happy existence spent working the fields during the day, and at night crowded into the two-room mud-brick house with its dirt floor brushed clean. The ancient blackened stove burnt fiercely in the corner, fending off the fierce frozen blasts from the Himalayan mountains, and providing the favourite meal of tsampa (roasted ground barley flour mixed into a dough with salted yak-butter tea) and mo-mos (dumplings).

Lama Yeshe's parents realized they had given birth to someone special when nuns from the Chi-me Lung Gompa (or convent), some two hours away by horse, began to take an unusual interest in him. It had been some years since their beloved Abbess had passed away and their approach to Nenung Pawo Rinpoche, a lama famed for his psychic powers had directed them towards the house where Lama Yeshe was living. He had predicted the exact time and place of Lama's birth. The nuns, having found their reincarnated Abbess, began to make offerings to the small boy and would often take him back to their convent to attend various religious ceremonies. Lama Yeshe was perfectly happy in this environment and often spent days away from his family in the company of the nuns.

During her lifetime the Abbess gained a reputation as a great yogini, gathering around her nuns with high spiritual attainments. Significantly, it was said that this Abbess's fervent prayer was that her work in this lifetime would enable her to be reborn in such a way that she could bring Buddhism to those in spiritual darkness, and those that no other lama wished to teach. In Lama Yeshe, her prayers were about to be fulfilled.

As a woman it was somewhat gratifying to know that the powerful figure I had met, had been in a female body such a short time before — women gurus being in as short supply in the East as they are in the West. Later, when I tackled the lamas about the glaring absence of female spiritual leaders they admitted that the whole monastic system in Tibet was geared towards fostering male authority figures but that there were, indeed, great women meditators who through their own brave, solitary efforts achieved the highest possible goals.

One of Lama Yeshe's most appealing characteristics was that he was deeply sympathetic towards women and clearly understood them. Indeed at times he seemed almost to become a woman. Not that he was ever effeminate, but he could, if the situation demanded, metamorphose himself into someone who was undeniably 'soft', 'gentle' and 'intuitive'. Consequently women responded to him and instinctively trusted him, sensing that he knew what it was like to be a woman. It was a rare quality to find in a man, especially one who was also indisputably masculine. Lama had become the essence of the true spiritual being, one who had developed both male and female qualities to the full.

From a very early age Lama Yeshe expressed a desire to lead a religious life. He later said that although he loved his parents dearly, he felt that their existence was full of suffering, that the life of the householder did not offer true happiness, and it was not the path he wanted. Whenever a monk visited their home he would beg to be allowed to leave with him and join a monastery. Finally, when he was six years old, his parents relented and took him to the mighty Sera monastery, one of the three great monastic universities near Lhasa, where he was put in the charge of an uncle who was a monk there.

Sera monastery, four kilometres along a dusty track leading out from the capital, is similar to the other major monasteries in Tibet in that it is totally unlike any other establishment on earth! Imagine a vast walled city climbing up a mountainside with huge painted figures of Buddha sculpted into the boulders above. The city is a maze of different-coloured different-shaped buildings, all combining to make one brilliant coherent whole. Its symmetry, when analysed, is a masterly product of the asymmetrical. Here are tiny, winding alleyways, minute doorways leading unexpectedly into courtyards where you find perpendicular wooden staircases leading to a labyrinth of rooms beyond. These are the monks' cells — minute, head-high, dirt-floored and pitch-black, not only from the lack of windows but from the fires constantly burning to keep the salted yak butter tea perpetually on the boil. A butter lamp flickers in a corner, illuminating a holy picture and a low platform bed covered with an ornate Tibetan rug. Nothing else. The whole place seems encrusted with a thick layer of tar accumulated from centuries of ingrained dirt, incense and candle smoke. Washing, either of things or bodies, is not high on the list of priorities in Tibet! To all intents and purposes you could have entered the cell of a medieval alchemist.

But if the rooms are dark and dingy, the outer walls of the buildings and the temples dazzle with a blaze of colour — scarlet, royal blue, emerald green, sunshine yellow, gold, silver and precious jewels. Here Tibetan artistry has found its highest expression in the exquisitely ornate woodwork, carvings, brass fittings and, of course, the statuary. The Buddha figures, which emerge from the artists' hands after months of meditation and thus transcend the boundaries of the personal egotistic imagination, festoon every inch of the temple walls and rise into the vaults of the ceilings, often 60 feet high, so that you have no choice but to raise your eyes to look into the face of the Fully Awakened One, gazing down at you with the serene smile of compassion.

In this ancient ordered world, infused with the power of intense spiritual activity amassed over centuries, Lama Yeshe was to spend 19 years of his life. Cut off and caring nothing for life outside the monastery and Tibet, he was perfectly content.

'It was a wonderful place. So sacred,' he once explained to me. 'I lived in Sera with over 10,000 monks and life was very disciplined. It was said that not even a flower was allowed to grow in Sera in case it distracted the mind! Anyway, we had to wear robes with both arms bare at *all* times. You can imagine what that was like in the winter! And the schedule was hard. The day started at 5 a.m. with morning puja (prayer ceremony) and then we had pujas throughout the day until 7 p.m., with three hours free from 12 to 3 p.m. In the evening we had to memorize texts in order to keep the scriptures continually in our minds. Then there would be debating and testing of the texts regularly. It was quite hard work. If I got to bed before 11 p.m. it would be early,' he said.

'Sera, of course, was an educational monastery,' he continued. 'I had four teachers teaching at different levels. The emphasis was on philosophical matters like understanding the true nature of reality, Emptiness, and the Middle Way, the fundamental Buddhist doctrine of avoiding extremes. But I also had many meditational masters who taught us how to meditate on the quality of human life, how to utilize this precious human birth, and what to do during death, as well as many other subjects.'

Lama Yeshe was never particularly well known among his countrymen for his academic record. He did well, especially in debate, but was known more, even then, for his humility and loving kindness. He never took his geshe degree (equivalent to a doctorate of divinity) even though he had been studying for it since he was 12. When asked why not, by a western student, he retorted 'What and be called Geshe Yeshe – how ridiculous!' In fact I heard another story, probably much closer to the truth. His uncle had once offered him the money needed to sit for this examination but Lama Yeshe had turned it down, saying it would be better spent feeding the poor. Instead he'd gone off and done a three-year silent retreat with his special lama. To all outward appearances he remained 'an ordinary monk', which was just the way he liked it.

Lama Yeshe continued his recollections about Sera: 'We talked about nothing but Dharma all day. And that is what we enjoyed. My every need was taken care of by the religious community. I wanted for nothing. If you leap into the discipline it is a very peaceful life. It was, it seemed, a totally secure environment. I thought I'd start and end my life there!'

He could have had no inkling of what was in store. His knowledge of the West was confined to the talk of old men, who unanimously described 'the red-skinned foreigners' as barbarians, lacking in even the basic form of spirituality. Lama Yeshe wasn't entirely convinced. He once saw a white man in Lhasa and took a good look. 'He seemed very intelligent to me. Later when I began to teach and live with westerners my own people were shocked. They thought I should not mix with foreigners, believing we were completely different. But I never felt that way. I felt western people and me were the same. This is my karma, and so I let go,' he told me. Was this the product of an unusually broad mind, or the deepest desires of the former Abbess speaking? Maybe it was one and the same thing.

His world was literally blown wide open with the Chinese invasion of his country in 1959. Much has been written about the anti-religious fervour that gripped Mao Tse Tung's Red Guard as they stormed into Tibet, ransacking the monasteries, destroying priceless works of art, imprisoning, torturing and killing many monks and high lamas. It was more than the end of an era, it was the brutal annihilation of arguably the last great ancient culture left on earth. What was being destroyed under our very noses was a rich and rare civilization comparable to that of ancient Egypt or the Incas. The world stood by and watched. Doing nothing.

With shells exploding all around him at Sera, Lama Yeshe, aged 25, made the first major decision of his adult life. He decided to flee. And so, due to the forces of destiny or karma, the closed secret world of Tibet was forcibly wrenched open, and its greatest treasure of all, the pure and complete teachings of Mahayana Buddhism were finally given to the rest of the world. As Lama explained later: 'I realized I had to go. Even if I had stayed I would not have been allowed to continue my life as a monk, and that if I wanted to carry on studying and practising I had to leave Tibet. Having made that decision I intuitively knew that Lhasa and the monastery were over for good. I cried. Friends said I'd come back but in my heart I knew that wasn't true. Saying goodbye was terrible. My sister clung to me, begging me to stay, saying I could stay hidden at her house. I knew that was not possible. I didn't dare say goodbye to my mother. It would have broken her heart.'

Taking off the robes he had worn since he was six, Lama Yeshe donned lay clothes and with two brothers he began his escape over the vast, inhospitable Himalayan mountains. He walked all the way out, carrying his few belongings on his back. Now, for the first time in his life he had to beg for food and face real hardship. At night it was so bitterly cold that he would light fires in a circle all around him, but it did little to stave off the sub-zero temperatures. Every time a band of Chinese soldiers approached, a Tibetan would run ahead and warn the three monks. It took Lama Yeshe over a month to reach freedom in India.

It was freedom of a sort. Lama Yeshe, along with hundreds of other Tibetans who'd escaped, was interred in a big grim, refugee camp in Buxaduar, North-East India. To the sheltered, naïve and simple monk, the world he found himself in was bewildering. 'It was a *big* shock,' he confided. 'Actually I thought I'd gone immediately to hell. India seemed so degenerate in comparison with Tibet. The heat was unbearable, so was the food. I hated rice and dahl, loathed the smell, and it made me sick for months with terrible stomach trouble. And for the first time in my life I had to think of life in terms of money. I never thought of money in Sera! Now I began to realize that anything that needed to be done had to be done through rupees. From knowing nothing about such things I had to learn fast. Actually the Chinese were very kind – they forced me to meet the outside world, and truly test the Dharma. I could have spent the rest of my life meditating, but that's not good enough. A monk's life should be used for others,' he said.

The fantastic discipline engendered over nearly 20 years at Sera monastery began to pay off. In their refugee camp the Tibetans set up the teaching programme once more and continued their studies. Along with classical texts, Lama Yeshe delved into poetry, and much to his peers' disgust, English. During this period he was habitually late for his 9 a.m. debating session. He was late because he overslept. He overslept because he was awake all night learning English. He'd frequently deny this, if asked, but his classmates often caught him with an English primer. They told him it was a waste of time and that if he wanted to learn a second language he'd be better off with Hindi. Lama carried on regardless.

About two years after he had entered Buxaduar, a young reincarnate Lama called Zopa Rinpoche came to him as a disciple. For both of them it was a turning point. Lama Zopa Rinpoche, who was to play such a crucial role in the drama that was about to unfold, had a formidable personal history himself. He was born in 1946 in a small village in the Solo Khumbo region of Nepal near Mount Everest. As a small child he used to play 'gurus', giving initiations to his band of tiny followers, but no one took much notice since in this part of the world such a game was about as commonplace as 'cops and robbers' in the West.

What did catch his parents' attention however, was his repeated attempts, from the time he could crawl, to traverse the precipitous paths up the mountain to a cave that had belonged to a famous meditator called the Lawudo Lama. Time and time again he had to be forcibly retrieved. The Lawudo Lama had spent the last 20 years of his life devoting his time to spiritual practices, and had given advice and teachings not only to those people who came to his cave seeking guidance but to the other yogis inhabiting nearby caves. Before he died he'd promised to return in a younger, fitter vehicle to do even more for the people of his region. (True to his word, Lama Zopa set up the Mount Everest School for Sherpa boys, currently flourishing at Kopan.)

When Lama Zopa was three he disappeared for one entire night. Frantic with worry, his parents organized a search party. His uncle finally found him in the Lawudo Lama's cave, declaring stubbornly, 'I am the Lawudo Lama, even though nobody will believe me.' He further insisted that he wanted to continue his life of meditation and prayer. The uncle, finally convinced, promised to establish the young child's status officially. Accordingly he was subjected to a public examination by a master of the Nyimgma sect of Tibetan Buddhism, Ngawang Samden, who lived nearby. The child passed and was finally recognized as the true reincarnation of the Lawudo Lama.

Lama Zopa continued his school-life until the day his uncle decided to take him on a pilgrimage to Tibet, carrying the young boy most of the way on his back. Arriving at the Dung-kar monastery in North Sikkim, home of the famous Domo Geshe Rinpoche (immortalized in Lama Govinda's classic book, *The Way of the White Clouds*), Lama Zopa startled his uncle by announcing that he was going to stay. The uncle understandably objected, but when the commissioner of the region intervened and said the young boy's wishes should be respected, the uncle returned home alone. Lama Zopa once again got his own way.

If life had progressed smoothly Lama Zopa would have met up with Lama Yeshe at Sera monastery, where he planned to go for his further education. As it happened he too was forced to flee from the iniquities of the Chinese invasion, and he made his way to Buxaduar where destiny finally caught up with him.

One day in 1965 an extraordinary thing happened. Into their room burst the most unlikely figure of all. A beautiful, young, blonde 'princess' of Russian descent, by the name of Zina Rachevsky. She was looking for the Domo Geshe Rinpoche, no doubt inspired by the romantic figure of Lama Govinda's book, and was taken by mistake to Lama Zopa, who was also known as Domo Rinpoche ever since his stay at Dung-kar monastery in Tibet. Unaware of the mistaken identity she strode forward and boldly asked: 'How can I receive peace and liberation?'

To say the two lamas were startled would be an understatement. No foreigner, especially the dreaded western 'barbarian' had ever entered their quarters before. No 'barbarian' had ever spoken to them like that before. And certainly, no 'barbarian' had ever talked of wanting enlightenment.

But then Zina Rachevsky was no ordinary person. Her life was, in its way, every bit as extraordinary as the two lamas'. Her father was a Russian prince, a Romanov who had fled the Russian revolution, her mother an heiress, one of the richest women in the United States. Zina was brought up in Hollywood, and became a typical product of Tinsel Town – spoilt, precocious, insecure, attention-seeking, deeply unhappy. By the time she was a teenager she'd already hit the headlines more than once, not only for her entrée into the world of starlets, but also for her involvement in various drug scandals. She was gorgeous, curvy, sexy, a Marilyn Monroe lookalike, wild and determined to live on the edge.

With the arrival of the 1960s Zina was ripe for the flower-power movement of 'peace and love' – especially the latter. She had numerous affairs and several husbands, one of whom happened to be Conrad Rookes who made the film of *Siddhartha*. She began travelling, living with a colony of artists on the Greek island of Hydra, and then moved on to the hippy mecca, India. It was while she was in Sri Lanka that she read *The Way of the White Clouds*, and with a determination that came from always getting what she wanted in life, she decided that the Domo Geshe Rinpoche was somebody she *had* to meet.

By the time she met Lama Yeshe she was, quite bluntly, jaded. The drugs, alcohol, late nights, rich living and too many sexual entanglements had taken their toll. To the lamas, she must have justified their countrymen's every prejudice about the degenerate, unspiritual, western devil. And so for a while they said nothing, merely looked.

Was she real? Was she a fraud? Or was she, as Lama Yeshe suspected, someone very special? With his more mature wisdom he decided to test her. He explained to me: 'I gave her some sort of answer, with my limited English, and after an hour she said she had to leave. To my surprise she asked if she could return the next day. I said "all right". And she did come and asked more questions, and I gave teachings. For one week she made the journey by jeep to see us, and then asked if we'd be prepared to go and visit her.'

Lama Yeshe hesitated for a moment. The step he was about to take was irrevocable. At this point Lama Zopa stepped in. With all the zeal of his youthful Bodhisattva's heart he begged Lama Yeshe over and over again not to forsake this woman who had come seeking his help. Lama Yeshe still demurred. Did Lama Zopa know what he was asking? Could he be aware of the enormous responsibility that they were about to initiate and which would one day fall solely on his shoulders? Was he prepared for all that was on the verge of being brought into effect?

But the Bodhisattva promise, which they had both taken, is written not in sand, which the tide can wash away, but hewn out of rock and stands for all time. They both knew, of course, they could not refuse anyone sincerely seeking the truth. And so Lama Yeshe and Lama Zopa set the wheel of Dharma turning for the West, and daily for nine months gave Zina Rachevsky the teachings she so earnestly desired. It must have been a mutually fascinating exchange. If Zina was intrigued by the holy men she had stumbled upon, they must have been transfixed by her. As Lama Yeshe told me, 'She was very dissatisfied with everything! She said her life was empty and had no "taste". She'd done everything in life, but still could find no satisfaction. I could see what she was saying. In comparison I had nothing – no country, no home, no money, no possessions, no family, and yet I had everything. With Zina, and later with other westerners, I began to enquire about their lifestyle. I realized that what Zina lacked was an understanding of herself, her inner life. She lacked an understanding of her own potential to be happy. She thought happiness came from without, but it does not, it comes from within.'

Zina had finally found the meaning that had been lacking in her frantically sad life. When her nine months of private tuition were over, the expiry of her visa forced her to return to Sri Lanka. She then bombarded the Dalai Lama with letters entreating him to give Lama Yeshe and Lama Zopa permission to visit her in Sri Lanka. When permission was granted, Zina returned to India to escort her lamas, but on the spur of the moment decided to go with them first to Dharamsala to try and get an audience with His Holiness personally. Once there she became convinced that her true vocation was to become a nun. Again Lama Yeshe was stopped in his tracks. Having a western female disciple was one thing, having one with a shaved head and red robes was another. 'I thought about it for a while,' he admitted, 'then decided it was all right! It even seemed a good idea. So I asked the Dalai Lama personally if he would ordain Zina.'

The link being forged between the lamas and the West was growing stronger. Lama Yeshe now had to consider what was the best thing for a newly ordained American Buddhist nun. 'I thought about going to the West with her, but decided the time wasn't right. And so the three of us went to Nepal, which is next to Tibet. Nepal is very beautiful, which I thought was important for Zina and myself. Being ordained in itself was not going to be enough for her — what she required to support her in her new life was simplicity, plus peace,' he said.

The strange triumvirate made their way to Boudhanath, a few miles out of Kathmandu, the picturesque town surrounding the great Stupa, with its all-seeing Buddha-eyes painted on all four sides surveying the lush green fields and brown terraced mountain slopes. It is the most famous shrine outside Tibet, and consequently has become a focal point for many a devout pilgrim. Here, amid the religious artefacts displayed in the tiny shops surrounding the Stupa, the dirt, cows, goats, beggars, monks, swirling prayer wheels, beating of gongs and drums, the three found a house and settled down.

In due course some of Zina's friends came looking for her and were drawn by their own curiosity and the obvious change in Zina, to hear what Lama Yeshe had to say. They stayed. More people came. As time passed and numbers grew, Zina purchased the land on a hill overlooking Boudhanath and the great Stupa. Its name was Kopan. The birth of a phenomenal movement had begun. The time was absolutely right. Zina Rachevsky, in spite of her anarchic and unhappy past, had ignited a mighty fire which continues to burn strongly to this day.

Once a nun and ensconced in Kopan it would be wrong to give the impression that Zina was completely transformed. Thirty-five or so years of a certain lifestyle cannot be totally eradicated overnight. From time to time her autocratic manner would surface, and rile the early settlers at Kopan, all of them hippies and none of them taking kindly to authority. Age Delbanco, a Danish man, who was enticed to stay at Kopan after Zina had promised him she could fix his visa problems with the Nepalese Immigration Department, remembers her clearly: 'She'd issue a lot of orders, which no one would follow and she'd get really mad. She wanted us to think of her as a mother, but really we could only think of her still as a princess! She had a fierce temper which would arise from time to time, and she was hopeless with money. She couldn't handle it at all – like a lot of rich, spoilt people. But she was also full of enthusiasm and loved the lamas so much. She had a very big heart.

'The last time I saw her she'd just emerged from a three-month retreat and was transformed. She was beautiful, absolutely radiant. Calm and peaceful with a sweetness pouring out of her. It made me see that a lifetime's habits can only be got rid of slowly – she'd only known the lamas about one and a half years, not long to change the mental habits built up over 35 years. But she was trying! After that retreat it showed.'

Zina's dramatic life continued to the very end. She was to die suddenly at the age of 42. Some say it was hepatitis that killed her, others that she died of food poisoning.

Knowing that the only course for Zina was more retreat, Lama Yeshe had sent her to a cave in the Himalayas where she was to spend three years saying some 3,600,000 mantras, among other spiritual duties. She'd agreed, understanding that this was the best path for her. Initially she'd found the isolation and seclusion terrible. She was lonely and frightened, and spent much of her time writing her diary. But this had gradually worn off, and Zina entered the spirit of the retreat and became happy.

When she was almost halfway through, Lama Yeshe awoke one day at 6 a.m. at Kopan, and insisted on being taken to the airport. He had to see Zina, he said. The journey to her cave was either 10 days by foot or a couple of hours by plane. The monsoon season had just begun, however, and flights in and out of Kathmandu were difficult. Arriving at the airport, Lama Yeshe discovered that no flights were scheduled and there was a long queue of people waiting to go precisely where he was heading. Undeterred, he waited. When the flight was eventually announced Lama Yeshe, with uncharacteristic pushiness, literally forced his way to the front of the queue, throwing aside all those in his way (mostly burly Sherpas). He stood in front of the counter and demanded a ticket. The Sherpas, astonished at such behaviour from a lama, stood mutely by. He got his seat.

Lama Yeshe spent 10 days with Zina and then returned to Kopan. She passed away six weeks later in great pain but in the meditation posture, which she maintained for several hours. Although he had told no one the reason for the urgency of his visit, he had known that this was the last chance he had to get to his first western disciple before the rains came and made the journey to her cave impossible. He had to reach her before she died. He knew the enormity of what she had done and what he owed her.

That's not the end of Zina's story. The finale is told by another one of Lama Yeshe's students, Christopher Kolb, who coincidentally was doing a retreat in Lawudo, Lama Zopa's birthplace, at the time Zina died: 'I was living in a remote hut with a tin roof, and these crows would land on the roof and tell me if anyone was approaching. One day they thumped on the roof very hard, began squawking and doing an intricate dance. I figured it must be someone really important who was coming. Soon a runner arrived and told me that a famous rinpoche from the Mount Everest region wanted to meet me at a certain point. How this rinpoche knew who I was, or where I could be found I didn't bother to ask, having got used to the psychic powers of high lamas by now.

'I went to meet him and he told me that three days previously he'd seen in his meditation that Zina had passed away. He'd prayed for her over the coming days and on the eve he set off to meet me he'd had a dream in which Zina had appeared to him looking beautiful, wearing new clothes and full of vitality. He wanted me to know that she had gone to a pure realm and would take a very fortunate rebirth,' he said.

Although her early death was tragic, and shrouded in suspicion, she passed away at the peak of her life, and with the fire of spiritual practices in her heart. She could not possibly have been aware of the great movement she had started.

5

THE VISION

The prophecy made by the great eighth-century Tibetan saint, Padmasambhava, looked as though its time for fruition had come. He had decreed: 'When iron birds fly, and horses run on wheels, Tibetan people will be scattered like ants across the face of the earth and the Dharma will come to the land of the redskins.'

By the early 1970s planes were certainly flying overhead, there was a plethora of cars on the road, Tibetan refugees were spread across the globe and Lama Yeshe had begun teaching the 'redskins' (westerners) at Kopan. It was, it must be admitted, a far cry indeed from the structured, disciplined, religious community he'd known back at Sera. Those first disciples who found their way up the beautiful, peaceful hill from the dust and dirt of the Kathmandu Valley were a motley, fairly unsavoury crew – unwashed, unshaven, unkempt and mostly out of their heads on illegal substances. For months, sometimes years, these hippies had been on the trail in search of a good time, spiritual inspiration, or maybe just dope. By the time they reached Kopan most of them had been through the whole spiritual supermarket trip, shopping at various ashrams around India, gleaning an eclectic range of mystical snippets and eastern philosophies, forever on the great guru hunt. Lama Yeshe hardly balked. Instead he set to work transmitting his precious teachings to this most unorthodox audience with the dynamism and ingenuity that were to become his hallmark.

I managed to track down some of the first Kopan visitors to hear what it was like in the early days. Christopher Kolb, now 40 and helping to build a Stupa in Washington DC, cheerfully admits that he was one of the more extreme cases. He arrived at Kopan almost naked with hair down to his buttocks and ash smeared all over his body, in the style of the wandering Indian holy men, or Saddhus. He had a scarf tied around his head which read 'Om Nivah Shivaya', the universal Hindu mantra which praises Shiva in all His omnipotence. For the past year he'd been living by the ghats of the Ganges where the dead bodies were burned. He was tripping when he arrived.

Nevertheless the moment he saw Lama Yeshe he knew he'd 'come home'. 'The recognition of the great being he was, was instantaneous. And I was not on a guru number. I'd been round the block more than once,' he told me. 'I gave him my only possession, a shell mobile I'd bought in Goa. He took it and went inside his room to show Lama Zopa. I heard laughter, but when Lama Yeshe came out he was crying. His heart wept for the American boy from Utah.'

Lama's approach with Christopher was to shatter every preconceived idea he might have had about 'spirituality'. On the surface it seemed outrageous, but Lama clearly knew what he was doing. 'One of his first questions to me was, "If someone was coming to Nepal with a nuclear bomb to blow everyone up would you kill him?" After all the talk of love and kindness towards all sentient beings it was quite a turnabout. Lama's own answer was that I had a *duty* out of love to kill the murderer. It shook me wide awake. A second remark following fast on the first was: "You hippies sit and watch the sunset and think it's beautiful. To me the sunset is ugly." I sat in mute amazement. Then Lama went on to explain himself. The sunset, when analysed is "mere appearance", transitory, offering no lasting happiness. It was precisely the kind of goal a lot of us were pursuing,' Christopher admitted.

Lama Yeshe was using unconventional means to break through the lassitude and anarchy of his first followers. His outrageousness appealed to them. He was, in his own way, every bit as controversial as they were. And by not compromising his message, not couching it in sweet words, he invariably hit home. Christopher Kolb was dissatisfied at heart with who he was and the life he had been pursuing. He continued: 'Part of Lama's genius was that he spoke your mind. He put into words thoughts that you had only half formalized.'

Lama never softened his approach with Christopher. At every opportunity he would single him out for what appeared to be harsh treatment – criticizing his appearance, publicly pointing out his faults. Christopher didn't mind – he'd at last found a man he could love and respect. He decided to become a monk – with all the discipline and denial that entailed. Still Lama didn't relent. He was not about to let Christopher's new-found religious commitment be the means for shirking his worldly responsibilities. Although he was separated from his wife and two children, who had gone back to Europe, Lama made him write to her and ask her to come and live with him at Kopan, and keep them. The only catch was that Christopher had to maintain strict control over his vows, including celibacy. It was the hardest task Lama could have set, but Christopher accepted. The family thus stayed together living happily albeit unconventionally in Kopan for a number of years.

In gathering his first flock to him Lama wasn't always harsh. Most of the time he was the exact opposite, showing a tolerance, kindness and love that was truly exceptional. For one 18-year-old, Steve Pearl, he trekked all the way across Kathmandu to accept an invitation for dinner, issued largely out of curiosity. Steve took him to a nearby dive and then because it was late offered Lama his spare bed – the seat out of his car. He had no blankets. Lama said nothing but covered himself with his robes. It was only years later when Lama was visiting California, where Steve now works as a commercial pilot, and they were dining together in an expensive Japanese restaurant that Lama teased Steve about their first date.

'He was so humble,' recalled Steve. 'I was too young and naïve to know that you didn't behave that way with a special lama, but he understood.' Steve, like so many thousands to come, was magnetically drawn to him. 'I knew he was really special from the moment I set eyes on him, but I fought it. Subconsciously I recognized that he would change my entire life.' After hearing him teach, Steve had gone to Lama to seek advice about a medical problem. Lama duly directed him to a good Tibetan doctor. Steve decided to stay clear of any further dealings with Lama Yeshe. 'But the day came when I knew I had to go to him. So I went to his house in Boudhanath where he was living with Zina, but he wasn't there. I was told to wait. I got so nervous just sitting there that I decided to meditate, which actually was the best thing I could have done before a meeting with Lama. Eventually he came and said, "What can I do for you?". What came out was, "I wanted to thank you for helping my body and I was wondering if you could do anything to help my mind?" As I said it this warm glow started to spread through my heart. It was utterly blissful, like nothing I'd ever experienced before. Lama didn't say anything. He just sat there.'

Still resisting, Steve left Lama and decided to travel to India, where other Tibetans were, to see if all lamas had this effect on him. Perhaps it was a trick they'd learnt in Lhasa. After months of testing other lamas, the experience hadn't happened again and Steve returned to Kopan.

By this time the building had begun. First to go up was the main temple, or Gompa, under the protective branches of the huge Boddhi tree which dominates the courtyard outside. Gradually over the years the rest of the buildings followed to accommodate the ever-growing stream of visitors and residents attracted to this magical place. Steve set to work building his tower, an enchanting three-floored edifice, complete with ornate pagoda-style roof — financed by money he'd received in compensation for a road accident in the States.

The flamboyant Max Matthews, a black American woman who was to have a very close relationship with Lama Yeshe, was another prominent early pioneer. She was a high liver with a reputation for drinking any man under the table at the smart Yak and Yeti hotel in downtown Kathmandu. When she got married (against Lama Yeshe's advice) she hired a plane and threw rose petals down on the marital home. A few months after the wedding ceremony the marriage was over and Max went to Lama declaring that she'd decided to become a nun. Lama Yeshe just said 'Yes, dear,' as though he'd known all along that this was her inevitable course and he was merely waiting for her to realize it.

With his own hands Lama Yeshe made her golden blouse to wear under her maroon robes which, next to her black skin, made her look more dashing. He then put her in charge of the young Sherpa boys who were arriving to attend Lama Zopa's Mount Everest School. She became known as 'Mummy Max', a title that she has kept to this day. It has gathered added significance since then because Max kept working, first as a teacher, and latterly as a businesswoman, handing over her entire salary to support Lama Yeshe and his work. Still a nun, she now has an exclusive dress shop in San Francisco, patronized by an élite clientele who are not at all deterred by the small altar just inside the front door containing a picture of Lama Yeshe, her mentor.

At the beginning Lama would send Mummy Max off to Kathmandu in the jeep to continue her teaching job. They were happy days, informal days. Lama Yeshe had time then to mingle with his students, forging bonds of friendship and intimacy that were denied to those who arrived at Kopan later, when his work took him far afield. It was these early settlers, the first ever to encounter Tibetan Buddhism, who were filled with the zest and energy required to create the huge Foundation that was to follow.

As Nick Ribush, an Australian doctor who renounced his medical career to become a Buddhist monk after meeting Lama, told me in London recently, 'My memories of those early days are only good, although there *must* have been some bad moments. It was like discovering a diamond mine. There was such a high coming into it. I was getting answers to all those questions that I'd never bothered even asking anyone before because I knew they didn't have the answers. The meaning of life – and all that. Meeting Lama Yeshe and Lama Zopa was very mind-opening. They were very accessible then, not as they are now. There weren't so many people around and we spent hours with them. The thing was we offered ourselves in service to them from the very beginning. We did so without any sense of loss, only gain. So we worked with them very closely right from the start and were involved in all the developments that were to follow. We were extremely fortunate,' said Nick, who is now director of the publishing company Lama Yeshe inspired, Wisdom Publications.

So Kopan took shape, with Lama Yeshe (who loved flowers with a passion) planning, planting and tending the gardens which continue to flourish and give pleasure to this day. Until he found a chef whom he trained, Lama also cooked for everyone. His entrepreneurial skills in this direction, as in every other, soon became apparent. Sensing that his students were feeling somewhat homesick he asked them one day what they would eat for breakfast in their own countries. They duly gave him a mouthwatering description. A few days later they emerged from their beds to find that Lama had erected a stall in the courtyard just outside the Gompa and was busily preparing the breakfasts of their choice: freshly squeezed orange juice and crunchy muesli for the Americans, cooked eggs for the British and Australians, fresh bread with cheese or jam for the Europeans. How he duplicated the food from mere description, having never seen such breakfasts before, was only less remarkable than his love for his followers which prompted him to perform such an act. After two months of personalized breakfast service, the students decided they didn't need it any more to help with their meditations.

In every respect Lama Yeshe made them feel at home. He didn't want them to feel that they had to renounce their own cultures in order to follow what he was saying. It was a theme he constantly reiterated in many forms. For instance he personally built a small pond with a fountain outside the Gompa, after he'd learnt from an American girl that that was the kind of feature an American would put in his home to make it special.

But the highlight of it all was the teachings. The first proper meditation course given to westerners was in November 1971. It was a month long, and was based on the 'Lam Rim', or 'The Graduated Path to Enlightenment'. Twenty people attended – living mostly in tents they pitched on the hillside. By the second course the numbers had risen to 50, by the third they had swelled to 100 and by the fifth to a colossal 250. The November meditation course that I had gone to had become an annual tradition. In spite of their limited English and poor pronunciation Lama Yeshe and Lama Zopa must have been doing something right. Lama Yeshe in particular was homing in on the minds of his audiences, discovering their propensities.

'As I saw more and more westerners I realized they were intellectually advanced. They easily understood the Buddha's teaching. What they lacked, however, was an experience of the teachings which they could only get from meditation. Only when they learnt to meditate would they know they had reached the truth, and then from that inner experience they could put their intellectual understanding into practice in their everyday life,' he told me.

He began to gain a clearer idea of what it was that had turned these young men and women into hippies, rejecting the cultures of their own countries. 'I felt that western civilization was set up in such a way that material values were the great things in life. Nothing else was as valid. That made me sad. I realized it wasn't anyone's fault, I'm not blaming anyone, it's just set up that way. This, I think, leads to unstable minds, fractured minds. Human relations don't seem to hold together so well. That made me unhappy,' he continued.

'I believed that Tibetan Buddhism had something valuable to offer westerners. Western people lack an understanding of the function of consciousness. They don't know the capacity of human beings – that they can achieve things beyond this world. They can reach incredible states of happiness through their own mind. I felt maybe I could explain this in such a way that people got a glimpse of what is possible. So I try to give an introduction into the possibilities of their inner world,' he said.

And all the time Lama Yeshe was developing his own highly individualized style of teaching – breaking with the traditional format to couch the essential meaning, what he called the nuclear energy, into modern western parlance and a late 20th-century context. It was a bold stand on his part, one that brought raised eyebrows and implicit criticism from his countrymen, but one which won him thousands of western followers. As I found out from the purist stance that Lama Zopa took with the scriptures, Tibetan Buddhism in its strict written form is dry, medieval and anachronistic. It seems as palatable, and as relevant as Hobbes's *Leviathan*. Lama Yeshe's delivery – witty, vital, shocking, pertinent and absolutely relevant to today – delighted and captivated his audience. It was his great gift.

As he said, 'Our teachings are not secret doctrines, but I had to think of how I could put my Buddhism in a western way. The Tibetan method is slow and full of historical references. Nagarjuna said this . . . Shantideva said that . . . westerners needed something more concrete, something they could relate to their own experience. I couldn't change the Buddha's teaching, but I had to find a way to get it across. It is quite a challenge! I daren't have any fixed plan. Each time I talk to people I have to check what background they're coming from. Are they religious, or non-religious, scientific, non-scientific, philosophical, or just ordinary? Then I try to talk according to their language. It takes a lot of energy. But Buddhism adapts itself to this because it is essentially about human beings, and teaches you to go beyond limited philosophical concepts.

'Take karma, for example, which is a huge subject. So complex. Because westerners have been brought up in a totally different framework from Tibetans they can approach karma from a completely opposite standpoint. If you're not careful you can have a big argument on your hands because you're both coming from different directions, and both arguments can be logically argued. I try to go beyond the philosophical framework to the essence of Buddhism, the "nuclear energy" and try to put that into western minds. Actually so long as I don't lose the essential meaning, I don't care any more about the philosophical structure,' he stated bluntly.

His link with westerners well and truly forged, the next stage of Lama Yeshe's work began to take shape. It was to be vast in vision and implication. The culmination of his life's work. By the mid-1970s many of his Kopan students had found their way back to their own countries, but found that the inner peace their meditation course had given them rapidly evaporated on contact with the demands of their own environment. Consequently they asked Lama Yeshe to visit them and give the teachings within the context of their own culture.

Lama Yeshe knew what this implied. 'I shook a little bit,' he said. 'Such a simple monk going to the super-samsara world. But I accepted their invitation.' (Samsara means the deluded world suffused with suffering.) In 1974 Lama Yeshe took his second big step into the outside world. Accompanied by Lama Zopa and the American disciple Max Matthews he went first to Indiana, USA, to visit Louis-Bob Wood, who'd found her way to Kopan after seeing Lama Zopa's face on her TV screen when it was switched off. She didn't know who it was but certainly recognized him when she reached Kopan. She'd organized a meditation group and was eager to get a booster from the lamas.

The next stop was Australia, where news of the lamas' arrival had spread, drawing 200 ex-Kopanites to Diamond Valley, 60 miles north of Brisbane, Queensland. It was a phenomenal success. When it was over, the participants decided they wanted to establish a permanent base. Four people who'd purchased land near by at Eudlo, as an investment prior to travelling to the East, generously donated it to the cause. Other students offered money, many more offered physical help in clearing the land, and building. The centre was duly erected, in the style of a typical Queensland house, on stilts and with a verandah all around. It was small – just one main room for meditation and teaching, and two smaller rooms, one for storage and one to house the resident nun who was to be installed immediately. The Chenrezig Institute (named after the Buddha of Infinite Compassion) was born. It was the first in a long line of such centres.

The following year, Lama Yeshe was invited on a second world tour, the biggest he was ever to undertake. It took eight months and included Thailand, Queensland, Melbourne, Sydney, Los Angeles, Nashville, London, Switzerland and Italy. At nearly every stop Lama Yeshe was approached and his advice was asked on establishing a centre. He thought it an excellent idea.

'Each time I went to a different country my Nepal students said they wanted to be in a group, to have the support of group energy. I could see they were very sincere and their dedication strong,' he said. 'They'd all come to the East and put so much effort, such hard work into learning and meditating and within a month of returning it had vanished. I completely understood. They had "baby" Buddhism, "baby" Lam Rim, "baby" refuge. I thought what they were asking for was essential.

'You need the correct environment to allow concentration and awareness, especially in the middle of the polluted city. The centre itself therefore becomes a place of refuge. It's the same for me. I need to go on a strict retreat once a year so that my talk, my "blah blah blah" is useful.

'So I said to my students "OK, if that's what you want, but it's your baby. I let go."'

It was an attitude he often adopted, wanting to shake off dependence on the 'guru' and fostering instead independence and a sense of responsibility. 'We have to rely on our own *inner* wisdom,' he would often say. I'd seen him get exasperated more than once by students asking him questions on the minutiae of their lives – issues he thought better answered by common sense. 'You want *me* to dictate your life to you?' he once replied to a middle-aged Italian man who wanted Lama's opinion on whether he should return home or do a retreat.

Thrown back on their own resources, the hippies suddenly found themselves putting on suits, cutting their hair, and visiting bank managers, credit companies and estate agents. They were up to their necks in big business. Ironically they were often to be landed with real estate that was so big that it far outweighed the small problems of the semi-detached properties their conventional friends were dealing with. The mortgages, debts, and attendant building problems, were, of course, comparably bigger too.

Standing on the steps of Kopan Gompa in November 1975, Lama Yeshe gazed into the distance, as if surveying with his mind's eye the ever-expanding movement that was being generated under his very nose and said to Nick Ribush, 'We need an organization to keep all this together. Why don't you get a few people together and start thinking about it?' The group thus formed met on a regular basis.

Nick Ribush explained: 'We had all these theoretical models of how the organization should work, and spent hours *talking* about it. We'd then go to Lama with our suggestions which he would throw out, modify or accept. Although he was encouraging us to take on the responsibility for what we had asked for, he didn't want these new developments going off on tangents. The centres had to fulfil certain aims and Lama had in mind that they should last well beyond our lifetimes into future generations of Buddhists. For this they had to have a solid foundation from which they could grow.'

The name given to the organization was a mouthful – the Foundation for the Preservation of the Mahayana Tradition, a name which nevertheless encapsulated its function. The centres existed to preserve the principles and teachings of Mahayana Buddhism, that rich vein of ancient wisdom that had been dug out of Tibetan soil and was rapidly being transplanted in the West.

Lama Yeshe's vision was bursting into flower. This new Foundation was going to do its job in a number of ways: through city centres – where people could come after work, at lunchtime, over the weekend for meditation, relaxation, peace; residential country centres – to provide longer courses, short retreats, and a community where people could raise families in a spiritually motivated environment; monasteries to train and teach the growing number of monks and nuns who would be the teachers to come; retreat centres in remote areas for the truly dedicated meditators; a publishing company and many other off shoot activities to serve the community in various ways.

He saw the whole thing as a mandala, a unified whole with

Right: Lama Thubten Yeshe. Giving teachings he invariably emanated a potent mixture of profound wisdom and heartfelt compassion coupled with an unorthodox delivery and an irrepressible sense of humour.

Below: Lama Yeshe in one of his many unconventional guises donned to gain greater insight into our Western way of life and thinking, here enjoying the Californian beach with Geshe Lobsang Gyatso, the resident teacher at Vajrapani Centre, Boulder Creek.

Reincarnation — a major visible force within Tibetan Buddhism.

His Holiness Kyabje Ling Rinpoche, the Dalai Lama's senior tutor, who died in August 1983 in the full meditation position, and his reincarnation, Tenzin Choepa, aged two.

His Holiness Trijang Rinpoche, junior tutor to the Dalai Lama, in blissful mind three days before passing away, and his reincarnation, on the throne with bell and *damaru* drum, taking up his spiritual duties where his predecessor left off.

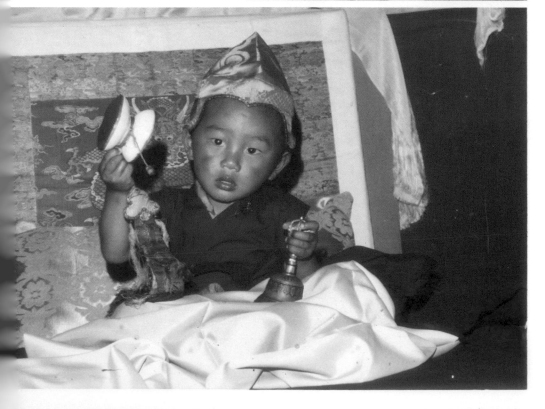

The most famous reincarnation of all, His Holiness the Dalai Lama, spiritual and temporal leader of Tibet and regarded by his countrymen as an emanation of the Buddha of Compassion.

Above: The 13th Dalai Lama, whose head turned after death indicating the direction of the place where he was to be reborn.
Left: His successor, the young reincarnation Tenzin Gyatso, the 14th – and current – Dalai Lama, discovered in 1935 in a humble family in north-east Tibet.
Below: The Dalai Lama today – no longer living in splendid isolation in the Potala Palace, but a citizen of the world urging peace.

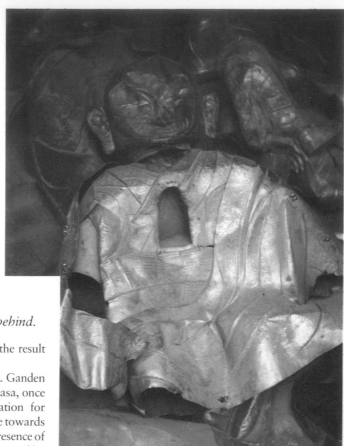

The world the Dalai Lama left behind.

Right: Desecrated Buddha statues, the result of Chinese revolutionary zeal.
Below: The destruction of old Tibet. Ganden monastery, 40 kilometres east of Lhasa, once the centre of learning and meditation for 5,000 monks, now in ruins. A gesture towards restoration has been made, but the presence of a mere 270 monks has yet to be sanctioned by the Chinese.

Left: Lama Yeshe in 1984 in California, where he went to die. His death, like his life, was a teaching on what is possible for human-kind to achieve. He was cheerful, joking and compassionate until the very second he passed away.
Below: Lama Yeshe's funeral stupa, lovingly built by his Western students – according to exact Tibetan instructions – on the land at Vajrapani Centre, Boulder Creek, California. Lama Yeshe's body was dressed in full cere-monial regalia and placed upright on the wood before being set alight.

a Yeshe's final message – 'everything is impermanent'. Was this the end of the Tibetan
her who had touched so many lives throughout the world?

Left: Osel Hita Torres, fifth child of an ordinary Spanish couple, before being recognized as the reincarnation of the late Lama Yeshe. *Below:* The meeting of the new east and west reincarnations. Osel and Trijang Rinpoche, who knew each other in their previous lives, greet each other again in Dharamsala and delightedly hand money offerings back and forth.

different aspects fulfilling different functions. It would serve the needs of different people at any one time and also serve the individual at different times in that person's progress. It was, in Lama Yeshe's words, a vision of 'universal totality', and as such it was to provide for far more than spiritual needs. Lama wanted to create the setting for a universal family, welcome in whatever part of the world it happened to be. He wanted to smash not only the false barriers of nationality but the creed of individualism, so highly regarded in the West, which he saw leading to loneliness, isolation and a fundamental lack of joy.

In one moving talk he gave to the students at Lama Tsong Ka-Pa Institute in Pisa, Italy, he summed up his feelings: 'At the moment we have such a narrow concept. We think "He's Tibetan", "I'm Italian", and so we don't have a world vision. That's the wrong attitude! Everybody not believing in everybody else's way. We should instead create a universal system. This centre should belong to everyone. Not just to Italians and certainly not to Lama Yeshe. I don't want it. This centre belongs to the world community. There should be no walls. Then you are practising Boddhicitta,' he said.

Today that aspiration has truly been realized. Nearly five years after his death the FPMT continues to expand at a remarkably fast rate. There are now 50 centres and affiliated organizations spread across 15 countries, including Nepal, India, England, Spain, Holland, Italy, France, Germany, the USA, Australia, New Zealand, Singapore and Hong Kong. Most centres have a resident Tibetan Lama, originally dispatched by Lama Yeshe, and several monks and nuns. Although each centre is financially responsible for itself there is a Central Office in Kathmandu which acts as a link between the centres and Lama Zopa Rinpoche, who now heads the organization. And, as Lama Yeshe wished, there is much contact between his family members, with FPMT students travelling frequently between each others' centres and feeling instantly at home.

Apart from the centres there is the highly successful publishing company, Wisdom Publications, with its home off Bond Street in the heart of London's West End. There is also the monastery Nalanda, near Toulouse, France, which provides an intensive study programme for the steadily increasing number of monks. The new Root Institute in Bodh Gaya, India, (where the Buddha gained enlightenment) has a whole range of facilities, including a leprosy project for the area as well as an agricultural, handicrafts and educational scheme. Because of India's role as source of the teachings and her continued kindness to the Tibetan people, Lama Yeshe wanted the Root Institute to help preserve India's own wisdom and culture in all its varied manifestations, while encompassing the Buddhist ideals of universal responsibility and education. In Australia a Buddhist hospice movement is starting, and tentative steps have been taken to start schools in Europe. Lama Yeshe continues to reach out to thousands.

But if the prophecy of Padmasambhava was coming true, it was not just the 'redskins' who were benefiting. Tibetan Buddhism itself was getting a face-lift. It was, some would argue, badly needed. Tibet, although totally spiritually motivated, had because of its isolationist policies run into the very real danger of becoming stultified. There was much superstition and in some quarters corruption. Lamas had been known to succumb to bribes to announce a child a rinpoche – the family receiving much status and material benefit as a result. Nor did all monks have a true vocation – many went to the monastery because it afforded a secure way of life and education. On a mundane level, the man in the street was content to turn his prayer wheel and do his prostrations before the image of the Buddha, rather than open his texts and gain some enlightenment from the profound wisdom they contained.

The beauty of Buddhism is that its truths can only be found through sincere and constant personal enquiry. Tibetan Buddhism, rich and complete though it was, needed a blast of fresh air. Had the Chinese not invaded it was, perhaps, in danger of becoming, like the dinosaurs, too weighty and complacent to continue to live. Coming out of its closed world, it encountered the fresh, questioning ears of the West. In fact, the Dalai Lama himself once told an English friend of mine, that Buddhism now has all the vitality it had during the Buddha's own day when he was presenting it to open, sceptical minds.

Consequently, in grafting Tibetan Buddhism on to the West, Lama Yeshe was not interested in transporting its culture and ritual, the aspect which captivated so many of his followers. He told the same students at Pisa: 'Custom and culture are not important. Buddhism has travelled in the past to many countries

– China, Thailand, Burma, Tibet and has taken on different forms. Tibetan culture can never become Italian culture. I notice some students even try to become Tibetan. It's a joke,' he said derisively. 'They'd be much better off becoming Buddhist.' He went on to suggest serving spaghetti at their religious ceremonies. 'You have to develop Italian Buddhism,' he insisted.

He certainly believed that the cultural aspects of Tibetan Buddhism were not strong enough to deal with the problems of western life. It was meditation and understanding the philosophy which would, he said, bring about a real improvement in people's lives. 'The time is right for Buddhism to come to the West. There is so much mental suffering in the West – maybe because you have so much physical comfort. The monkey mind has to find something to occupy itself with! But it's the essence of Buddhism that must be brought over. And this essence must be related to western psychology, science and philosophy. Otherwise there's no connection. Actually this is not such a difficult job – the major Buddhist teachings such as the Four Noble Truths, the Eightfold Path, Shunyata and Boddhicitta are extremely logical and practical. They apply to people of all time, because they deal with fundamental human nature and the issues of suffering and happiness.'

Lama Yeshe was right. The remarkable interest in all forms of Buddhism that has suddenly sprung up in the West suggests that this profound, 2,500-year-old philosophy of the human psyche still has much to offer modern man.

6

THE RETURN

In the autumn of 1983 a close friend I'd met literally the week
after my return from Kopan, who had watched with interest my
steadily growing ·relationship with Buddhism, asked if I would
consider going back and taking her with me. It had been six years
since life had catapulted me into that very special monastery in
Nepal, and now seemed the appropriate moment to retrace my
steps, to see if that catalytic experience would repeat itself and to
introduce someone else to that rich, difficult adventure.

So once again I took the taxi from the airport through the noisy,
dusty streets of Kathmandu and climbed the rough road to Kopan.
It was reassuringly familiar. The large frangipani tree was still
blooming, the prayer flags were fluttering in the warm daytime
breeze, the brightly coloured little birds still darted between the
trees and the great kites circled noiselessly overhead. I had forgotten
how breathtakingly beautiful it was. There had been changes too.
A quick glance showed that the colony of dogs had grown; so had
the monks. There were now nearly 100, all dashing about in
their red and gold robes, shouting mantras, sweeping the paths,
memorizing their texts, playing football – an unusual life. The
facilities had expanded too, to accommodate the growing number
of people who had 'discovered' Kopan. There was now a dining
room, and many more rooms including some very small single
and double ones. We were given one of these, and much to my
astonishment it contained beds – two raised wooden platforms
with thin but discernible cotton mattresses on them. The window
even had glass. I explained to my friend that this was luxury indeed.

But the bath was still cold water and a bucket; the loo a hole in
the ground. That excruciating timetable with enforced 36-hour
periods of silence also remained. This time I relived my original
horror at the schedule and the hardships through the eyes of my
friend. She too went through the gamut of emotions induced by

those long hours of meditating, when mind-watching brought you face to face with the reality of your own mind. This happened to me too, of course, but now I was shored up by the confidence that the outcome was truly worthwhile.

While I shared in my friend's discomfort, I also participated in her moments of delight, standing on the hillside at dawn, watching the sun rise over the Himalayas to reveal the Kathmandu Valley below, shrouded in mist like some Chinese silk screen come to life. And that mysterious silence broken only by the plaintive cry of the big black crow who daily materialized on the post next to where we stood, cups of tea steaming in our hands. I remembered T. S. Eliot's lines: 'Go, go, go, said the bird: human kind cannot bear very much reality.'

Once again I listened to the teachings of Lama Zopa, thirstily drinking them in, not realizing how much I had grown to respect this patient, exquisite human being whose quiet personality was overshadowed by the dazzling brilliance of Lama Yeshe. Confidently I reassured my friend that in spite of the cough and odd pronunciation he would make a lot of sense if she persevered and tuned in. And so, of course, he did.

And I waited, without much hope, for Lama Yeshe to come and wave his magic wand over the proceedings and whisk away the doubts, fears, contentions and questions of the 100 or so people who had been drawn to Kopan and had so diligently rendered themselves up to all it had to offer. We had been told he was sick and was recuperating in retreat in Dharamsala. My heart sank – it could not be a true Kopan experience without the powerful presence of Lama Yeshe.

But come he did on a cold, bright December morning, two days before the end of the course, to the welcome of trumpets and conch shells being blown from the golden roof-top of the Gompa. The small monks had lined the road in welcome and had drawn the auspicious signs of Buddhism in coloured sand on the path. The jeep drove in, Lama got out, and a tangible silence fell over everything. No one said a word. It was somehow holy and terribly poignant. Something was happening. This was so very different from the joyful pandemonium that normally characterized Lama's homecoming. Lama Zopa, his face sad beyond words, stepped forward with the traditional white scarf or 'katag' in his hands.

They looked at each other with secret knowledge. Many of us were crying. We didn't know why. How were we to know that we had just witnessed Lama's last entry into Kopan – the base he had founded and from which his life work had blossomed forth?

Just as before, he walked into the tent, his kind open face all smiles, saying 'thank you, thank you', as he weaved his way between us to the raised brocaded seat where he sat, having done his prostrations to the Buddha.

I could see immediately that he was very ill. His eyes had lost their bright shine, they had bags under them and his skin had a greyish deathly pallor. He looked absolutely exhausted. My heart went out to him. And yet the same laughter. The same effort to put us at our ease. The same indefatigable wish to explain, to make it all clear. As if he were perfectly well, he answered questions for four hours, stopping occasionally to ask if *we* were tired and wanted a break. Here was his final gift, the living embodiment of all that was most precious in the teachings, the giving of all to others. The annihilation of the ego.

At one point, in answer to some question on identity (the perennial question on Emptiness), he pulled at his cheek, picked up the skin on his arm, thumped his chest and said 'Who do you think I am? Am I this face, this arm, this body?' Once again he had us grappling with the business of labels, and querying our habitual concept that only the concrete, the visible, the material is real. It was an answer I was to remember often in the years to come, when faced with Lama Osel.

On the last day he chose for his discourse the teachings on Bodhicitta – compassion. What else? Another four hours of tireless outpouring on the importance of love, and putting all others before self. 'Everything you have you got from others. You come from the mother naked, with nothing. No clothes, no speech, no food, no reading, no writing, nothing. All your happiness comes from others. True? This is not some crazy Tibetan philosophy. This is scientific. You check up. Bodhicitta in my observation is the essence of all religion. Bodhicitta is the most worthwhile thing. For western people it is the best way, the easiest way. Sitting cross-legged meditating is not western-style. Loving kindness is western style, because of your Christian orientation. Western people have that energy. So Bodhicitta is very simple, very logical for you western people.'

He went on to qualify what he was saying with the Mahayana Buddhist view that compassion can only be truly effective when one has got oneself in order. 'How can one drowning man save another? At the moment we have the wish – "I want to help others." I want to help my mama, my papa, my husband, my girlfriend. But with my mad elephant mind how can I help? It's a joke.

'My speech is a disaster, my actions are a disaster, my mind is a disaster! I want to help my mama, but I am worse than my mama. First I have to correct my own mind, then I can help my mama, my husband, my girlfriend. So I must try as much as possible to control my own negative mind, to make a transformation, to make myself satisfied and happy. This is the way to help all humanity.

'We must meditate. We do have compassion, but we need to find a way through meditation to emanate our loving kindness into universal love.'

Lama was as compelling as ever. Once again he had crashed through the barriers of culture, race and creed to reach the universality of the spiritual message. It was the perfect ending.

Just before he finished talking I slipped outside to try and catch a few personal words with him on his way back to his room. This time he was too ill to grant one-to-one interviews.

He took my hands, looked with intense care and love into my eyes and asked how I was. It was preposterous. Here was I so visibly fit and well, and Lama so ill and spent after his marathon talk.

'Oh no, Lama, how are you?' I enquired.

'I am well, dear. I have been on retreat and now I think if I take things easily I will be all right,' he replied, refusing to discuss his obvious state of ill health. Still holding my hands he continued: 'Tell me, is there anything I can do for you? Anything? Is there anything I can do?' He repeated the question several times, speaking from the heart. Love pouring out of him. Giving, giving. All he was interested in.

Moved, I replied that there was nothing more he could do for me; he had given so much already. But perhaps there was something

I could do for him. He paused and said, 'Just give my love to all my Dharma brothers and sisters', and walked slowly away.

It was the last I ever saw of him.

An hour later, just as I was getting ready to leave Kopan a messenger came, bearing a package for me from Lama. It contained some incense and a tiny statue of the Buddha. I had instructions to have the face painted. It was his final act of kindness, and, I like to think, a reminder of the final goal, and a token of the bond that had been forged between us.

7

LAMA'S DEATH

Some 20 minutes before dawn on 3 March 1984, the first day of the Tibetan New Year, the heart of Lama Thubten Yeshe stopped beating. He was just 49 years old. He died in a way that was every bit as remarkable as the way he had lived.

In retrospect it was curious that he had lived so long. His heart had three faulty valves and over the years had grown so large to fulfil its function that it now took up most of his chest cavity. By rights he should have died many years previously. As far back as the early Kopan days, western doctors in Kathmandu had said he had only months to live. Lama merely laughed. Defying common sense and medical opinion alike, he continued to hare round the world in pressurized aeroplane cabins, visiting his many centres and offering advice and teachings to his students at a pace that would have defeated any chairman of a comparable multi-national.

Once, when he was in England, I quizzed him about his medical condition and he replied: 'Ten years ago I was told I should have been dead by 50 doctors in Madison, USA, who were examining me. They couldn't understand how I was alive. They then gave me three to six months to live. I don't have faith in western doctors. If someone tells you you are going to die, what can you do except give up? I don't give up! What they don't see is that the human being is something special. We are beyond the ordinary concept of what people think we are.'

It was a theme he was particularly fond of: the potential of the human mind – so vast it reaches beyond our present comprehension. At every opportunity he hammered it home, understanding that westerners, for all their education and sophistication, were still hampered by ignorance of the scope of their own being, and were therefore plagued by unspoken feelings of limitation and low self-esteem. Lama knew the inherent greatness, the 'Buddha-nature', as he put it, that lies within each and every one of us. He knew because he had tapped it. 'Divine pride, dear, it's good to have divine pride,' he often admonished, which was not to be mistaken for ordinary pride, which by nature is false. He often used to say, 'Because you have such a limited image of yourself, this is the root of the limitation of everything – limitation of love, limitation of wisdom, limitation of compassion. You've already decided you are fundamentally narrow, so your whole life becomes narrow, your wisdom and your love, because you've given yourself this narrow projection.'

How, I had asked, had he kept alive all these years? 'Through mantra and the mind,' he said matter-of-factly. 'Controlling the body, you know, raising the body heat, that kind of thing is easy. So simple. It comes from the mind. The difficulty, however, is in controlling the mind,' he concluded, roaring with laughter.

Lama's mind control was clearly colossal. He'd suffered no fewer than 200 heart attacks, and although we all knew he had a 'heart problem' none of us ever guessed how ill he really was. The public face was always one of extreme vitality, dynamism, never-ending energy – perpetual giving. In fact, in private he was often exhausted. Nick Ribush, who accompanied him on his first world tour in 1971 remembers how one afternoon after Lama had pushed himself, meeting all those who wanted to see him, he'd come home and collapsed on the nearest bed, not having the strength to make it to his own. It was, he said, a cruel shock.

Significantly, the end for Lama began the night after he had given his all, delivering that four-hour discourse on love and compassion on 10 December 1983 to the students at Kopan. He was physically spent. His heart now began to malfunction seriously. He couldn't breathe, started to vomit and feel great pain. Deeply worried, his students rushed him to an intensive care unit in Delhi where he stayed under close medical observation. Technically he was diagnosed as having 'congested heart failure', which meant that his heart was unable to pump enough blood to the rest of his organs so that they in turn also began to fail.

He stayed in Delhi at a private house to recuperate for a month, and then, on the spur of the moment, made up his mind to fly to California to be cared for by his American students, of whom he was particularly fond, and receive the latest western development in coronary care. It was, to say the least, an unorthodox decision.

But then Lama had always been nothing if not unorthodox.

He knew full well he was dying. He'd told at least two of his American students the year before that he would not live to see his 50th year, and had even predicted the date to one of them – Losar (Tibetan New Year) 1984. The choice, it seemed, was his. While in Delhi he'd confided to an Australian monk, Max Redlich, that he could, if he wanted, live another two years. Later, Lama Zopa threw the entire band of followers into confusion and turmoil by stating that Lama Yeshe could have lived for at least another 10 years, but this was dependent on the prayers and karma of the students. Were we not worthy, not doing enough? We didn't know. Certainly there had been some dissent from the Manjushri Institute, Lama Yeshe's centre in Cumbria, England, which had upset him. And once in Kopan he had visibly got sicker and sicker, using sticks to walk with, until one day someone went to Lama Zopa and asked if Lama were dying, and he replied, 'Not if you do your practice,' whereupon Lama Yeshe miraculously recovered.

For whatever unfathomable reasons, Lama knew the time had come for him to die. In this light it would have been so easy, so natural, for him to have passed away in typical Tibetan Lama style – in a quiet place, meditating, amid familiar surroundings with maybe one or two spiritual masters near by. Peaceful and private. But he elected instead that his death be a very public, mechanized affair, and consequently the biggest teaching he ever gave on the potential of the human being and the meaning of love. Shortly before he passed away, while surgery was being contemplated, he told Lama Zopa, 'It doesn't matter whether the operation is successful or not, I have been able to use myself as a servant to others. I am completely satisfied with what I have done and not at all upset about dying.'

Between arriving at San Francisco at the end of January, and dying on 3 March, Lama was in and out of various hospitals, having tests and receiving advice on the best possible medical action. (An angiogram – a photograph of the heart using dyes – revealed that the arteries which serve the heart had, in Lama's case, not stopped at the base as normal, but had grown down and under and up the other side, taking on extra strength and size, and this was how he had kept alive. It was, said the authorities, quite exceptional.) Major heart surgery was duly recommended and

Lama insisted on going back to his house in Aptos, near Santa Cruz, on a beach with panoramic views overlooking the Pacific Ocean, to be looked after by his students.

This was his delight, sitting by his bedroom window, propped up with pillows, watching the sun rise and set over the great, thundering sea. Here with the devoted Lama Zopa, and his faithful attendant from Kopan, Thubten Monlam, he spent the last happy days of his life, surrendering totally to the care of his students. No other Tibetan Lama had ever done such a thing. It showed not only the extent of his trust, but the lengths he was prepared to go to in order to reach out to his disciples from the West.

'His kindness in letting us care for him until the very end was as much part of his love for us as his verbal teachings,' said Beverley Gwynn and Shasta Wallace, who I went to for a first-hand account of Lama's death. It was, of course, like nothing any of them had ever experienced before. None of them were to be the same again.

'We were ripe for nursing Lama, since we'd been with a very good friend who'd died of cancer just one month before Lama arrived. If we hadn't been through that experience we would never have dared to go near him,' continued Beverley and Shasta.

Happening so close together, the juxtaposition of the two events was very sharp. 'Our friend went inwards, she became withdrawn, overwhelmed by what was happening to her. A week before she died she gave up talking. Lama, on the other hand, although he was in incredible physical turmoil – not being able to eat, vomiting constantly, and sometimes writhing all over the bed – was somehow detached from his illness. He would say, objectively, 'Vomiting is so tiring', as though he wasn't involved. When our friend was in pain you'd know about it, but Lama never ever once complained. He wasn't "buying into" his illness as we would. He never registered pain.

'There was a lot that didn't make any sense. Lama Zopa was laughing a lot. We'd hear peals of laughter coming from him. There were moments when we'd be trying to feed Lama but he couldn't keep any food down and we'd be feeling desperate because he needed to build up his strength, and Lama Zopa would come and start to joke with him. Although we felt emotional, we never felt depressed. Lama Zopa kept saying he was only *manifesting* sickness. It made us question a lot. "Does it matter then if he is vomiting?" How should we relate to the whole thing?'

There were other curious aspects. Lama Yeshe didn't look pale and gaunt. He'd lost a lot of weight – his arms were wasted and small, he had a huge, barrel chest, he was withered and debilitated, but his face was always serene and beautiful. His skin, normally brown, took on a luminous golden hue. He never cleaned his teeth but his breath never smelt. Nobody felt squeamish or wanted to retch while he was vomiting – that didn't have any odour either. His eyes always had a twinkle in them.

The sick room at Aptos rapidly turned into a theatre. Lama Yeshe gave them all jobs to do. At times they were fairly menial, getting him water, massaging his legs, looking at his teeth, fixing his pillows, fetching him water – anything to stop them feeling inadequate. Realizing what was afoot, Beverley one day said to him, 'Lama, it's so wonderful to have this opportunity to serve you this way. I know it's very rare to be able to have this constant close attention with you. It's putting us through a lot of change. Is this why you're doing it?' And he replied, simply, 'Yes, dear.'

At other times the tasks were more arduous. Lennie Kronisch, a registered nurse, and a fairly recent student of Lama Yeshe was called in to help in a professional capacity. She recalled: 'Being with him was this extremely fierce and intense moment-to-moment process of total concentration, total investment in what you were doing, and total attention to what was going on. Personally he put me through some experiences to test how far I was willing to go. He took me to the ends of my physical, mental and emotional limits.

'For instance he had sleeping problems, which meant that he would take catnaps whenever the mood would come over him. Often, after we'd carried him to his chair by the window he'd fall asleep in a really awkward position, slouched sideways and I'd find myself kneeling on the floor with a pillow in my hands, supporting his head. He needed his sleep so badly, I thought I had to help him as much as I could. Often I'd get so tired in that position I thought my hands would break, or my knees or back, and just when I thought I couldn't stand it a minute longer he'd wake up and "release" me, so to speak.'

One day a similar thing happened, which was to have strange

repercussions when she met Osel. 'Lama Yeshe was sitting in his chair and fell asleep while I was feeding him. I was bent over him and he reached up and pulled me to him by my shirt. Then he fell asleep. I was absolutely stuck. I had a spoon in one hand, a glass in the other, and he was holding on to me by my blouse. I looked to see if he was putting it on, but he was genuinely fast asleep. I decided the only thing to do was to stay with the situation moment by moment. At the point when I thought it was unendurable he woke up.

'That's why he let us hang around till the end – to give us these inner teachings. I'd never gone to these extremes before, not even for my three children. I understood then that this was the purpose of a guru, to take you beyond your present limits. What he did for each of us was to show us our personal best,' she said.

Most of all, in this would-be dire situation, they witnessed the extent to which Lama Yeshe had renounced his 'ego', and was utterly without a sense of self. 'What was truly amazing throughout it all was his constant concern for other people. I remember once after he was being sick for a long time, which was so horrible to watch because it was utterly draining on his energy, someone came in the room and he looked up and said, "How are you? How is your family?". He meant it.

'He communicated with us all the time and was very loving. He'd embrace us all, very strongly, intensely. Sometimes he would just look into your eyes and you'd feel this great outpouring of love. It was like you'd found your true love. Remarkable. He was so sick, yet his energy was constantly going outward,' said Shasta.

The end drew nearer when Lama, still at his house in Aptos, suffered a stroke. He was taken immediately to the local hospital in Santa Cruz, which for some reason best known to himself, he hated. He grabbed Lennie by the hand and in a voice of unmistakable command ordered, 'Get me out of here.' He repeated this demand every time she went near him. She was torn between her medical training and her devotion to her spiritual teacher. Finally her heart won, she 'came out of the closet', as she put it, and set the administrative wheels in motion to get Lama discharged. They were not pleased.

Back in Aptos, paralysed down the left side, Lama Yeshe still demonstrated unusual energy. He had a triangular bar above his head for him to pull himself up with, and he used to *swing* on it, as if in fun. He was delightfully playful and teasing with those around him. Lennie taught him special breathing exercises to help him relax, and every time she went past he would let out a huge mock sigh, sending her up. He'd get bored, like a mischievous child, and throw Kleenex on the floor one after the other to amuse himself.

Lama Zopa, constantly by his side, decided it was time to call in the Tibetan authorities. He phoned Switzerland and asked His Holiness, Song Rinpoche, a leading light in the spiritual hierarchy, and one of Lama Yeshe's own teachers, to come to California. The venerable old man, then in his 80s, with the archetypal long white wispy beard springing from the point of his chin, duly arrived. He said prayers over Lama Yeshe, gave him initiations and read his ancient texts for the appropriate treatment of strokes.

Mantras were the prescription, and removing Lama from all sources of direct sunlight. So one of his last remaining pleasures, sitting by his window watching the sun on the ocean, was removed from him. He was withdrawing from this life. Curiously (or perhaps not, according to your convictions), the paralysis began to show a marked improvement, but the congestive heart condition was plainly getting worse. Three days after Song Rinpoche left, Lama began to go downhill.

When another student, who was a doctor, arrived to see him and immediately counselled proper hospital treatment Lama Yeshe genially concurred. Lama Zopa did some divinations and Cedars-Sinai hospital in Los Angeles was selected as the most auspicious place for Lama Yeshe to go. He was air lifted there by helicopter ambulance, which he loved, laughing and joking all the way.

As it happened, Lama Yeshe's final destination was as far removed from his roots as can be imagined. The intensive care unit at Cedars-Sinai hospital glitters and hums with the latest high-tech equipment western science has devised to help combat our greatest killer – heart disease. Imagine, if you can, this Tibetan Lama from one of the most isolated places on earth being brought to lie next to film producers and TV moguls all having their big time heart attacks in the most important coronary care unit in America, possibly in the world. Here Lama was hooked up to an impressive number of machines blinking and beeping overhead, and giving digital read-outs in the 'operations' room outside. Cedars-Sinai was cold, efficient, brilliant, plastic – the best and worst of what America has to offer.

If it was all foreign to Lama, it was even stranger for Cedars-Sinai to have a Tibetan holy man in their midst. Along with their patient came another small, intense lama in robes who sat in the corner saying prayers or doing full-length prostrations to the man in the bed. There were also a couple of other Tibetan monks, and an entourage of western followers all crowding into the hospital room, going through their rituals regardless of the starched white uniforms bustling around them. The place was buzzing with the exotic novelty of it all.

Lama was ceremoniously attached to a tube going into his nose, another going into his arm and another penetrating his heart. In spite of all this he characteristically treated his doctor, Stephen Corde, who he'd never met before, as though he were an old family friend, and continued to joke and laugh with all around him.

He was in intensive care for just two nights before he died. No one had any idea it was coming. On what was to be his last night he'd asked for a Chinese meal, and had already eaten some strawberries, discussing those he grew in his garden with the nurses.

On the way in, Lama Zopa had noticed a woman, clinically dead but being kept alive by machine. He shook his head and asked if such a thing could happen to Lama Yeshe. When he was told it was possible he murmured it was better that Lama Yeshe should die than have his life sustained in such a manner.

He then gave instructions to the hospital staff that if Lama's heart was to fail no extraordinary measures were to be taken. He must be allowed to die naturally. Then by a quirk of fate he decided to call Song Rinpoche again and ask his advice. Back came a reverse decision, 'to do everything possible that western science has to offer for Lama's benefit'. The forces of destiny were at play. Lama, at the last minute, was to have a fully westernized death.

But that was not before he requested Lama Zopa to go through with him his entire meditational practice on the self-initiation into the highest yoga tantric deity of Heruka – an aspect of the compassionate Buddha. When he had finished his heart began to beat erratically. A nurse monitoring the machines in the 'operations' room outside noticed the change and rushed in to ask if he was all right. 'Yes, dear,' he replied. 'Was he in pain?' 'No.' She went out. Then, without warning, his heart suddenly stopped. Lights went on, alarms went off, the door was thrust open, hospital staff tore in from all directions. All hell broke loose. One medic reached for something on a shelf above Lama Yeshe's head and the whole thing came crashing to the floor. Tom Waggoner, a student who was with Lama, experienced the most terrifyingly acute pain in his chest. The electric shock treatment began.

It was the rudest possible way for Lama Yeshe to die. According to all his religious teachings the cessation of the heartbeat does not signal death. It is precisely at this moment that the most important and subtle meditation on the journey of the consciousness out from the physical form begins.

Dr Corde had been working on Lama Yeshe's heart for two and a half hours, when a quiet voice from the corner suggested maybe it was time to stop. Lama Zopa could bear it no longer. The doctor looked strangely crestfallen. He later admitted he'd never worked so hard to revive a patient before. Although he hadn't known Lama Yeshe, he sensed he was someone special. It was ten minutes past five on the dawn of the Tibetan New Year – an hour when most great yogis pass away.

In spite of all that had gone on those last few weeks nobody could quite believe Lama Yeshe had died. Lama Zopa was visibly stunned with grief. 'I am very numb,' he said. 'I can't think of anything. These high lamas like Lama Yeshe, they do not fit us. Because of our small merit they do not fit.'

The students were equally shocked. They half expected him to sit up in the bed and wink. As Beverley and Shasta explained, 'You see it wasn't an ordinary death. He was laughing, joking and embracing us up to the split second when his heart stopped. He was fully conscious all the time. In this way he showed us that death was ordinary, nothing to be afraid about. His body was ill but his mind was perfectly at peace. Happy. By dying of coronary heart failure he showed us his humanity. What happened to him could happen to any of us. Just as we could identify with his illness and physical condition so we could identify with his state of mind at death. It was wonderful how he did it.'

But there was business to attend to. The students tried to get the hospital authorities to give them a room where Lama Yeshe's body could lie undisturbed for three days, according to Tibetan tradition. The authorities responded with fear, outrage and indignation. It was completely against health regulations to leave a dead body in a bed for that length of time.

Finally they called the medical director and got a reluctant bending of the rules. Lama could have a room in a little-used wing of the hospital until 10 p.m. that night. Even in death Lama was still not towing the line! In true western style two hospital orderlies arrived, attired in white pants, white long-sleeved gowns, rubber gloves, caps and masks to avoid contamination from death. They lifted Lama on to a trolley. It was explained to them that this was a most unusual situation and that according to the custom of the deceased, the body must be jarred or jolted as little as possible.

Then began the bizarre funeral procession down the long corridors of Cedars-Sinai hospital, conducted at snail's pace, led by Lama Zopa and the other Tibetans in robes saying prayers, followed by the western students and then Lama's body, covered by a sheet and escorted by the orderlies in their moon suits.

Left alone with his friends and followers, Lama, clinically 'dead' but his subtle consciousness still very much alive within his bodily form, continued his meditation amidst the murmur of mantra and prayer. He was still golden in colour and according to those who saw him looked beautiful in death. From now on Lama Zopa was to refer to him as 'Lama's holy body'. When the time for staying in the room was coming to an end Lama Zopa, with exquisite devotion, made three prostrations to his precious guru and closest friend, which were so packed with pure love it shook all who saw it. He then began to shout Heruka mantras very loudly and announced 'Now Lama's meditation is finished!' One or two students saw Lama Yeshe's head move under the sheet, although the movement was so slight they wondered afterwards if they were hallucinating.

They later got a coffin and permission to cremate the body on their land at the Vajrapani Centre which had been established in the late 70s. With the unconventionality which surrounded all these events, Tom Waggoner then placed the coffin in his pick-up truck and drove the body some 350 miles back to Boulder Creek, stopping en route to wash the mud splashes off it at a petrol station.

It might not have been the average hearse, but he wanted it to shine like a chariot.

News of Lama's death travelled across the world fast and people began arriving from all corners of the globe to pay homage to the man who had touched not only their lives but their hearts. He lay in an open coffin in the main meditation hall, golden in colour and emanating sweet odours. To this day, the coffin still smells sweet. Many lamas also arrived, including the indefatigable Song Rinpoche from Switzerland – this time to oversee the funeral arrangements.

The wind, which had been howling unnaturally in the days preceding Lama's death, stopped the moment he passed away, and an unseasonally calm and blue sky graced Vajrapani for days. The rains also stopped, allowing the cars of the visitors to climb the dirt track to the centre. The clarity of the air mirrored the unusual clarity of mind of those who had nursed Lama. It should have been a grim, depressed affair but instead the cremation turned out to be a festival, a celebration. A time of joy and peace.

There was, too, the odd moment of bizarre hilarity. It fell to Tom Waggoner to keep Lama's body cold. Not having had too much experience of this before, he over-zealously packed it with so much dry ice that it froze solid. He saw his mistake when it came to the day of the cremation and Lama, according to tradition had to be sat upright in a chair with his legs an arms folded up against his body. 'I had 140 pounds of frozen guru on my hands – turning blue – and I had to defrost him quick to bend his legs and arms. We had some chuckles. Lama taught us to keep a sense of humour,' he recalled.

The ground was strewn with flowers, and incense wafted through the air, as Lama Yeshe's body was placed in the specially constructed 'Stupa' (burial chamber) diligently built by his students at night by the light of car headlamps. His body was prepared for cremation. His knees were drawn up to his chest and tied with white offering scarves. His arms were crossed and the ritualistic implements of dorje (a small 5-spoked sceptre) and bell (signifying indestructible wisdom and compassion) were placed in his hands. He was dressed in his magenta and yellow robes. On his head was placed a triple-tiered black Bodhisattva's hat adorned with a crystal rosary, and his face was covered by a red cloth. Then his body, sitting upright in a chair, was driven in procession up to the ridge where the Stupa was. The site chosen had a spectacular view of miles of Redwood forest and the smell of the unseen ocean beyond. Lama Yeshe had loved this place. It was, he said, a 'magic land'.

When Lama was in place, and the remainder of the Stupa built up over him, the oil-soaked wood was set alight by a woman who had not met Lama in her lifetime, according to the Tibetan tradition. For three hours the ritual offerings were fed into the flames and all the while the deep stillness was only broken by the sound of chanting and the crackling of the fire. A chance photograph taken through a gap in the Stupa later revealed flames licking through Lama's burning skull – a grisly reminder of his oft-heard teachings that not only are we all impermanent but that true peace of mind can only come about through staring reality fully in the face.

As Tom Waggoner commented, 'We're all going to die, yet we're all afraid of death. Throughout Lama's death my Buddhist training helped me not to despair. I'd been taught over and over again that death is just the discarding of an old worn-out body and that consciousness goes on.'

Lama's body remained untouched for four days until Lama Zopa opened the Stupa to examine the relics of the body. All that was left was a part of the heart, the jaw and Lama's distinctive buck teeth. Once again everyone heard him say, 'Am I this flesh, this form? Who am I?' Certainly Lama Yeshe, in the form that we had all known him as, had ceased to exist. When all the visitors had gone, the residents of Vajrapani Centre were left with an exhausted emptiness.

The feeling was most poignantly expressed in a Chinese poem that Shasta gave Beverley:

'Spring Ends' by Li Ching Chao

The Wind stops.
Nothing is left of Spring but fragrant dust.
Although it is late in the day
I have been too exhausted to comb my hair.
Our furniture is just the same
But he no longer exists.
I am unable to do anything at all.

Before I can speak tears choke me.
I hear that Spring at Two Rivers
Is still beautiful.
I had hoped to take a boat there
But I am afraid my little boat
Is too small to ever reach Two Rivers
Laden with my heavy sorrow.

8

DEATH AND REBIRTH

What precisely was happening to Lama Yeshe during his death nobody with ordinary perception could ever possibly know. But on this question hinges the whole issue of reincarnation, according to the Tibetan tradition, and Lama Yeshe's reappearance as a Spanish child 11 months later.

The Tibetans have made arguably the most detailed and profound study of death that exists anywhere in the world today – expounded most commercially in that famous eighth-century work, *The Tibetan Book of the Dead*. In it, the journey of the consciousness (that part of humankind which has absolutely no materiality) as it separates from the body, and what it experiences en route, is graphically and systematically described. And so, as a matter of course, every Tibetan familiarizes himself with the landmarks of this inevitable voyage so that he will not be thrown into panic by the strangeness of it all. Instead he will be able to retain some measure of awareness and control to enable him to arrive at a worthwhile, and hopefully happy, destination.

To the simple Tibetan, the aim is simply to die with a peaceful disposition – that state of mind being deemed good enough to steer the consciousness through the rapids of death. For the advanced spiritual practitioner, however, the goal is far more ambitious. Having studied and trained the mind throughout life to a high pitch of clarity and refinement (often through long periods of total seclusion and silence), the Tibetan yogi uses death as his greatest opportunity to blast through the final obstacles to complete awakening, or Buddhahood. But with the Mahayana ideal of altruism – moved by that unbearable compassion for the suffering of others – he forsakes his rightful place in what we would call heaven in order to fulfil his promise to return again and again to this wheel of life and death and show each and every one of us how he did it. When a being has reached such a level of development it is said

78

that he or she can dictate the *exact* conditions of his or her next birth, choosing one that best suits his or her divine purpose.

Fantastic tales abound of the extraordinary feats lamas can perform when they die. It is common knowledge throughout Tibet that when Mao's Red Guards desecrated the tomb of one of their most famous saints Tsong Ka Pa, founder of the principal Gelug, or Yellow Hat sect, they found not only his body intact but his hair and nails still growing, five centuries after he had passed away. Some yogis go even further than this and elect to take their bodies with them. Tibetan history is full of those yogis who have achieved the 'rainbow body' at death (like Marpa the Translator) and who vanish into thin air, leaving behind the nails and hair.

Fortunately, since the Tibetans fled from the cruelties of Chinese domination, we outsiders have had the opportunity to hear about and occasionally witness some of their remarkable achievements at death. More than one Indian official is known to have stood agog at the sight of a Tibetan master sitting bolt upright in the lotus position, a beatific smile on his face and sweet smells emanating from his body, long after his heart and breath have stopped. And this is in the sweltering heat of the subcontinent's noonday sun when, by rights, a 'dead' person should be a festering, stinking mess only good for the funeral pyre. Living in London, I did not have the opportunity to see such miracles myself, but other westerners who have lived with Tibetans in India and Nepal have given full credence to their exceptional powers.

The tale of how the much-loved Kunu Lama died in northern India recently has been spread far and wide among Buddhist circles. He was revered by Tibetans as the greatest living spiritual master of the century, the only man to whom the Dalai Lama has been seen to prostrate. The Kunu Lama was in fact Indian and, having studied Sanskrit and Hinduism thoroughly, he renounced both his country and religion and travelled to Tibet to seek the answers which his own creed left unanswered. There he became an itinerant lama, quickly developing a fierce reputation for scholarship and debate. He fled the country with the other high lamas after the Chinese invasion, and returned to his native land.

At the age of 90 he could be found at the Sacred Lake in the exquisitely beautiful Kulu Valley (dubbed 'The Valley of the Gods' by tourist brochures) near Dharamsala, home of the Dalai Lama.

Getting increasingly frail and having contracted tuberculosis, he nevertheless decided to work his way up the Kulu Valley, visiting the monasteries he found on the way and giving long teachings when requested. It was now February, the coldest month of the year, and the Kunu Lama was so weakened by illness and old age that he couldn't move from his little retreat house in one of the highest passes of this mountainous region. Yet one night he got out of bed and went out alone, walking several hundred yards through the snow until he found a tree which he promptly sat under, and in the blistering cold, passed away.

No one found him until the following day, his body still in the traditional meditation posture. It seemed impossible that such a sick old man could have done such a thing in those appalling climatic conditions, but perhaps the possibilities of the human mind go beyond our present concept of what is 'reasonable'.

There are other stories that have reached me over the years, all enthralling, all capturing the imagination. The well-known Apo Rinpoche, from Manali, for instance, said to be a reincarnation of the famous fifth-century poet-saint Milarepa, died of stomach cancer without showing any signs of pain. He was noted for his mastery of 'powa', the transference of consciousness technique which enables the accomplished practitioner to eject his consciousness at will into whatever form he thinks most suitable for his next purpose. Apo Rinpoche's body stayed warm for 14 days after his heart had stopped beating, until his own teacher arrived from Darjeeling and announced that his pupil's final meditation had now finished. At that, a trickle of blood left Apo Rinpoche's nostril and his head dropped to one side. This was the outer sign that his consciousness had indeed just left its physical form. It seemed clear that Apo Rinpoche had been fully aware of all that had been happening around him, and was only waiting for his teacher to initiate the last rites before taking his ultimate leave of this life.

Perhaps the most touching tale I heard was that of His Holiness Serkong Rinpoche. I had been fortunate enough to meet this remarkable man when he was staying at a friend's house in London. I was invited to have dinner with him and was immediately struck by his extreme 'ordinariness'. With no sense of pomp, and absolutely no ceremony (in spite of his high status within the Tibetan hierarchy) he sat at the kitchen table in the skirt of his under-robes and a pair of bedroom slippers, eating mo-mos (Tibetan dumplings) with an appetite that can only politely be described as 'healthy'. He urged us all to do likewise, until we were all utterly defeated. This 'ordinariness', I later learnt, was a quality he deliberately cultivated. He'd often choose to travel third class in Indian trains, a mode of travel literally comparable to riding in a cattle truck. Indeed, he would sometimes arrive to give teachings in a truck. A man of his standing was entitled to a chauffeur-driven car, but he didn't like ostentation.

In fact there was nothing ordinary about Serkong Rinpoche at all. Physically he looked like an extra-terrestrial, his face a relief map of wrinkles and deep furrows. His eyes were hooded, and gleamed with the 'wisdom gone beyond'.

His spiritual claims to fame were equally impressive. In Tibet he'd gained his Geshe degree (equivalent to a doctorate of Divinity, but a 14-year process) at the precocious age of 23. He was also rare among his countrymen for having a complete understanding of the four schools of Tibetan Buddhism, all of which are extremely complex. This meant that he was one of the few people who could prompt the Dalai Lama while he was teaching, and this was apparently a show worth watching. When teaching, the Dalai Lama rattles along at a fantastic pace – he would then stop and ask Serkong Rinpoche for a word. To those watching it looked like an enormous game – the Dalai Lama testing Serkong Rinpoche to see if he was keeping up. He invariably was. Serkong Rinpoche's devotion to his leader was touching in the extreme – his eyes would fill with tears at the mere mention of his name.

Not long after I'd met him in London a letter arrived from India informing us that Serkong Rinpoche had suddenly passed away. It told of the strange circumstances in which he had chosen to die. One day while he was staying in the remote area of Spiti, in northern India, Serkong Rinpoche summoned an aged monk to him and said, 'This is a very bad time for the Dalai Lama. His life is in danger. If we could take this on to ourselves it would be very good. But, please, don't speak of this to anyone.'

Unbeknown to Serkong Rinpoche, the Dalai Lama was at that moment en route to Geneva where, as fate would have it, the Swiss authorities were unable to provide any police protection, since all their forces were being directed to Yasser Arafat who was arriving

30 minutes after the Dalai Lama for a PLO conference. It was, to say the least, an extremely vulnerable situation for the Dalai Lama to be in.

Back in Spiti, Serkong Rinpoche was discreetly taking his leave of the monks he had served for so long, cryptically telling them that in future they were to address all their questions and problems to the Dalai Lama himself. Nobody guessed what he was inferring. He then called the same old monk and drove with him to a house further up the Spiti valley. It was clear that the owner wasn't expecting him at all. Serkong Rinpoche went in, ate a little yoghurt and recited the entire text of 'Tan-che Leg-che Nyingpo' – possibly the most difficult treatise on Emptiness. He then asked the owner to put a clean white sheet on the bed, after which he lay down, exhaled a couple of times, and died.

The letter continued, telling us that after Serkong Rinpoche had passed away he remained meditating on the clear light of death that night and the whole of the next day and night until the following morning, when his consciousness left his body. At that moment rainbows suddenly appeared over the house and lights were seen on the hill where he was to be cremated. At the dry, dusty place where his body was ritually burnt, a spring burst forth from the rocks and started to flow. It is still gushing to this day and has been the cause of several healings.

The letter concluded that Serkong Rinpoche had done exactly as he had promised – taking on the difficulties that His Holiness was experiencing and giving his life-force in exchange. As things turned out, at the moment when Serkong Rinpoche was 'dying', Arafat changed his plans and decided to go to Geneva the following day. Serkong Rinpoche's selfless act was not unique. Why there should have been so many deaths at this time remains a mystery, but it was said that the concern Serkong Rinpoche had for the Dalai Lama was shared by many highly evolved spiritual beings.

Coincidentally, around the time that Lama Yeshe died, many other Tibetan yogis also passed away in an unusual fashion. Not long after Lama Yeshe's death, the man who had conducted his funeral rites, the venerable Kyabje Song Rinpoche also passed away. He had fallen ill in the summer months of 1984 but after many students and colleagues had begged him to live he recovered completely and continued his full schedule of teaching, studying and performing religious ceremonies.

Then, in the early morning of 15 November, Song Rinpoche mentioned that he had a slight pain in his chest. It seemed to go, as the day wore on, and he was well enough to eat a hearty breakfast, saying to his attendant as he removed the tray, 'This has been appetizing, completely satisfying, excellent. You have been extremely kind.' Shortly after 9 a.m. he declared to all around him that he did not have any of his former illness and then walked briskly to his sitting room. A few minutes later attendants found Song Rinpoche sitting absolutely straight, eyes closed, with no sign of heartbeat or breath. He had simply 'died'. They did not touch him but read the rite of self-initiation of the tantric deity Song Rinpoche had practised. He stayed in that position for three days. During the afternoon of the third day the weather, which had been absolutely still, changed. Strong gusts of wind blew and slight earth tremors were felt.

Song Rinpoche's body, dressed in complete initiation costume, was placed on a richly decorated palanquin and borne aloft by his students to the cremation Stupa. On the morning of 24 November the cremation chamber was opened and there they found Song Rinpoche's skull unburnt and a large quantity of relic pills which had not been placed in the chamber with him. Finally, and most spectacularly, when the lower section was removed everyone present, including some westerners, saw in the ashes two small, but unmistakable footprints pointing in a certain direction. This was evidence not only that Song Rinpoche meant to return but of where to start looking for him.

I began to realize, as I observed this mighty display not of death, but the defiance of it, that what Tibetan Buddhism was demonstrating was not so much reincarnation itself (which is a doctrine shared by most eastern religions) but the deliberate rebirth and recognition of Tibet's major teachers and spiritual masters. No other religion offered this. And so Lama Yeshe, Serkong Rinpoche and Song Rinpoche – or rather the continuity of their mind-streams – was coming back again and again. When they are recognized – and the search for them begins the moment their previous body is in ashes – the special knowledge that they have gained and developed is nurtured and brought forth to nourish and sustain their followers anew. The implication of this is even more astounding when you understand that their wisdom comes not only from learning but from direct personal experience of the truth. This is why these people are called 'realized' – because in them the truth has become real. And this is why a recognized reincarnated high lama is given the title Rinpoche, meaning 'precious one'.

There have also been some impressive written accounts by westerners of the lamas' abilities at death. Lama Govinda, a German who became ordained in Tibetan Buddhism, has written his personal testimony in his beautiful book *The Way of the White Clouds*. He recalls how in the 1930s the British Envoy to Lhasa, Mr Hugh Richardson, visited Dung-kar monastery in southern Tibet and saw the upright corpse of the famous meditator Tomo Geshe Rinpoche, Lama Govinda's own guru, sitting on his meditational seat and being treated as if he were alive. The Abbot of the monastery asserted that the body had been like that for weeks and it was to be more weeks before the body was entombed. Lama Govinda writes: 'The guru had made it known that he would soon leave his body which had become a burden to him. "But," he said, "there is no reason why you should feel sad. I do not forsake you, nor my work for the Dharma, but instead of dragging on in this old body I shall come back in a new one. I promise to return to you. You may look for me within three or four years."'

Tomo Geshe Rinpoche was as good as his word, as Lama Govinda explains in his book. He came back in Sikkim at the exact place the oracle in Lhasa had described. On seeing the search party of monks approach he called out, 'Father, my people have come to take me back to my Gompa', and from then on proceeded to demonstrate the rare spiritual qualities shown in his previous life. Installed once again in Dung-kar monastery, the four-year-old boy impressed all with his composure, his familiarity with the rituals and the speed with which he learnt his scriptures. By the age of 7 his tutors could teach him nothing further and so he was sent to Sera, in the capital of Tibet.

So what exactly, we might rightly ask, were Lama Yeshe and these other Tibetan spiritual masters doing at death? Simplistically, for it is a very complex procedure, they were waiting for and watching the various sensations and visions that, they maintain, accompany the separation of the consciousness from the physical form. The separation is a gradual process. First they would recognize that the body was becoming heavy and would wait for the mirage-like vision. Next the fluids of the body start drying up and the meditator sees a vision that resembles smoke. After that the heat of the body disappears and the meditator sees 'sparks' with his inner eye. Lastly the breath stops and with that comes the vision of the 'flickering candle'.

As Lama Yeshe once explained in a long discourse he gave on death and dying, the point of learning and delineating these visions is so that you can recognize them and not be frightened when they happen. 'You deal with these visions, these illusions. You identify them and recognize illusion as illusion, projection as projection, fantasy as fantasy.'

But this was merely the beginning. After the initial four visions have come and gone, the subtle consciousness still remains. Lama Yeshe was adamant on this point. 'We still have the subtle consciousness even when there is no breath. Western doctors think you're dead when the breath stops and believe they can now put you in the ice box! But from a Buddhist point of view even though you are not breathing you are still alive with four more visions to come,' he said.

These in turn are the white vision (like being in the light of the full moon) which fades into the red vision (like being in the glow of dawn), followed by the black vision (being in utter darkness), after which comes the ultimate peak experience – the clear light, which by its nature is blissful beyond words, and exceeds anything we ever experience in our corporeal form. Interestingly, the last two stages of death, as described by Tibetans, tally exactly with 'near-death' experiences reported in the West where those who have been 'clinically dead' have suddenly revived and told the tale. They all describe going down a long black tunnel and emerging into amazing light which fills them with extraordinary happiness.

But whereas most of us can't help but bask in the pleasure of the clear light of death, the accomplished spiritual practitioner uses the enormous energy it engenders to meditate on Emptiness, the ultimate truth which decrees that all phenomena, including the self, have no independent existence. It is said that the combination of bliss meditating on Emptiness is so powerful that it acts like nuclear fission, blasting away the remaining obstacles to the fully awakened state. Omniscient mind. Buddhahood, no less.

Once the clear light vision has passed, the ordinary being is propelled involuntarily, by the habitual forces of his mind into another state of 'becoming'. The Tibetans maintain that he has no true control over what or where his next life will be, since he has no control over the propensities of his mind. He is thus buffeted to and fro from one existence to the other, at the mercy of his desires and aversions.

The being who has complete mastery over his mind, however, is said to be able to direct his consciousness into whatever form he wills. He could, if he so wished, remain in the 'pure realm' experiencing unqualified bliss for all time. Or, if he were a true Bodhisattva he would hear the cries of others and would, of his own free will, choose to return again and again to help them. This is the noble Mahayana Path, the 'Great Vehicle' of Buddhism, the way of altruism which finds in its practical form and its highest practitioners so much in common with the real Christianity. The forsaking of the self, the loving of the enemy, the turning of the other cheek, the doing and working for others. It is, of course, the hardest way there is.

How far Lama Yeshe got along this path I was never in a position to judge. He certainly had an enormous presence and all the attributes of saintliness. But he himself never made any boasts of his spiritual prowess, preferring at all times to put himself on our level. When he spoke he invariably included himself in his advice, as for instance in his discourse on Emptiness, delivered with typical panache.

'We have to build up the Shunyata [Emptiness] experience, don't we? We have to build it up little by little. First we get the baby Shunyata experience, you understand, then the teenage Shunyata experience, then the middle age Shunyata experience, then the elderly Shunyata experience, then the Great Shunyata experience. We're talking about experience, you know, not some intellectual trip. Intellectual people think Shunyata should be *this* or *that* but the actuality is different from the intellectual talk. It has to be organic, something we build up slowly, slowly.'

And so it became clear that Lama himself *must* have realized the Great Shunyata experience. But he would consistently deny he had any spiritual attainments. 'I am not the highest realized man,' he humbly told students in California a few months before he died, 'but I am a dedicated one. I do somehow have the wish to dedicate as much as possible my life for others. Even though I am a humble monk you should feel that I am always with you. It is important.'

This was quintessentially his style and one that I and many others warmed to, preferring it to the self-aggrandizement I'd witnessed in some Indian gurus who made public displays of their psychic powers and openly stated their divinity. Somehow that never quite rang true and I was delighted when I came across the story of how the Buddha had defrocked a monk for performing a miracle in public, claiming that the greatest miracle of all was the transformation of the human heart.

Obviously, Lama Yeshe was thoroughly acquainted with the death process. He talked about it often. 'You don't have to fear that dying is something horrible, like a black hole that's going to suck you in and eat you. We think dying is a big deal – worse than losing a girlfriend, boyfriend, husband or wife,' he'd say, roaring with laughter. 'This is the wrong attitude! Dying is better than any girlfriend, boyfriend, husband, wife, because those people can only give you very little bliss. The death experience gives tremendous peace. At death, when the clear light comes, you are in absolute bliss which embraces universal reality, not your ordinary concrete conceptual reality. Meditators can stay in that clear light for many, many days, or months. It is possible, you know!'

He advised us repeatedly to be aware of what our mind was doing as we fell asleep, saying that the sleep process is very similar to natural death in that the gross unconsciousness of our waking mind sinks into the subtler consciousness of the dream state and then into deep sleep. 'At that time [deep sleep] your consciousness is in its fundamental state, you know, without the intellect. You don't have the political mind, the communist mind, the capitalist mind, the angry, jealous, proud mind. That is why when you get up in the morning your polluted concepts have lessened through sleep and you are a little bit clear. It is the best time to concentrate or meditate for that reason,' he said.

Personally I was never alert enough when I went to bed to watch my mind through the sleep process, but many Tibetan yogis are, preparing themselves for the big moment when actual death comes.

Friends with whom His Holiness Song Rinpoche and Serkong Rinpoche had stayed confirmed that their sheets weren't even ruffled.

Since none of us truly knew the full extent of Lama Yeshe's spiritual prowess, we had to rely on his closest friend and colleague, Lama Zopa, to tell us. Normally it is strictly against spiritual etiquette to discuss either your own or another person's spiritual development but this taboo is lifted when someone passes away. After Lama Yeshe died, Lama Zopa gave a moving tribute to his guru, which gave us some indication of the magnitude of the man who had been with us those few short years.

'Most ordinary people who didn't know Lama's level of mind didn't realize that he was a great hidden yogi. He always used to take a rest after lunch for one or two hours. Wherever he was he would do this. At first I thought it was just an ordinary rest, but gradually I realized these were Lama's meditation sessions. At these times he would continue to practise his meditation on clear light. Lama was a secret yogi – he never slept.'

He went on to drop hints of Lama's other spiritual achievements. He had overheard him once say casually in conversation to another yogi that he had realized Emptiness, while debating in the courtyard of Sera monastery in Lhasa, when he was still young.

'Lama had such great will, such incredible dedication to work for others. He planned great projects for the benefit of others and to spread the teachings. Not only did he visualize this, he actualized it. He ensured his plans were accomplished . . . Lama's mind was open, you see. His heart was open to all traditions, all religions. He had such a broad view and could see far into the distance. He was not on a narrow path. He was not like those who tie themselves to the mountain by a rope afraid of falling off.'

He continued: 'Among Bodhisattvas there are those who have a stronger will to work for others. Shakyamuni Buddha, for example. When he was a Bodhisattva he actually gave his body to the tigers because they were hungry. So Lama had the power to control his life, to live longer than was thought physically possible. His power was due to his tantric realizations and his great Bodhicitta. He did this to guide us students, to help us make our lives more meaningful, to lead us from confusion. Lama said that for some beings even breathing became an act for others. What he meant was that alongside teaching and other normal activities even the act of breathing in and out could be transformed into an activity to help sentient beings. As he was saying this I felt he was describing himself.'

Lama Zopa concluded by revealing that in tantra, the most profound and complex of all meditative practices, whereby one ultimately actualizes oneself as an enlightened being, Lama Yeshe was also a master. Perfecting his tantric practice over the years he managed at the time of his death to initiate himself into the Buddha Heruka and so passed away in the sublime state of experiencing great bliss and Emptiness.

And so we assume that in that highly mechanized, impersonal room in Cedars-Sinai hospital, Los Angeles, Lama Yeshe summoned his considerable mental forces to utilize the great potential that the death experience has to offer. And when he was done, his mind residing in that blissful clear light, he looked about and found the best possible vehicle into which he could project his new form: the vehicle that would best enable him to carry on his great work – pulling down the barriers between nations and creeds in order to show human beings the much vaster universal wisdom and happiness that lie within.

9

THE BIRTH

On 12 February 1985, in the state hospital of Granada, Spain, Osel Hita Torres was born. He came into the world without causing his mother any pain, his eyes wide open. He didn't cry. The atmosphere in the delivery room was charged – very quiet and yet momentous. The hospital staff were unusually touched. They sensed that this was a special child.

Outside the heavens opened. Maria, the mother, lying with her new-born child, was scared. Lightning flashed, the rains poured down, filling the streets with so much water they looked like a river in full flood. This was the first time she had been alone at a birth. Her four other children had been born at home, which was how she liked it, but for some strange reason she had been advised by a Tibetan lama to have her fifth child amid the gleaming technology of a modern hospital. In spite of all the apparatus and the cold formality of the hospital ward the birth had been ridiculously easy. Just one contraction and the baby had been there. Now she was alone waiting for her husband, Paco, to come. When he arrived he took one look at his son and said with some awe, 'He's so serene, his face is full of light.' Maria suggested he find a name for him. When he returned the next morning he said he was to be called 'Osel', which means 'Clear Light' in Tibetan.

This was the child who was destined to become one of the most unusual spiritual leaders of his time. For Osel Hita Torres was soon to be officially recognized by the Dalai Lama himself as the reincarnation of Lama Thubten Yeshe, who had passed away in California 11 months earlier. It was later said that it was typical of Lama to engineer both an archetypal western death and an archetypal western birth – just for the experience.

From the moment they took Osel home to their small house, built by Paco himself, in the simple, charming village of Bubión, high in the Alpujarra mountains, Maria noticed that he was not like her other children. He never cried. When she forgot to feed him because she was busy with her other children, she'd race upstairs to find him lying in his cot wide awake, looking and waiting. He let her sleep all through the night, every night, from the day he was born. It was as though his entry into the world was not intended to cause inconvenience or trouble to the family in any way.

In fact from the time he was born Osel seemed to bring them luck. For the past six years, life had been tough for Paco and Maria – with so many mouths to feed and money extremely scarce. They were badly in debt and the strain was beginning to tell. Theirs was a good marriage but the relationship was beginning to crack under the strain. Now a new hotel was to be built in Bubión and Paco found work as a builder. He worked all hours and the money came in fast. Soon they were able to add more badly needed rooms to their cramped house. The strain lifted. Life suddenly began to improve. For a baby who wasn't wanted, Osel wasn't doing too badly. But this unpretentious, hard-working Spanish couple had no idea of the galvanic changes their new-born son was about to bring to their lives.

Paco and Maria had met on the island of Ibiza in 1976. Paco, a shy, self-effacing man, with a gentle, kind face and piercing blue eyes, came from a poor family and had left school at the age of nine to work in a factory. Later, seeking something more from life, he had thrown in his job, gone to Ibiza and met François Camus, a Frenchman who had met Lama Yeshe and Tibetan Buddhism on his travels in the East. Paco listened to what François had to tell him, intrigued at first, then deeply interested. Maria, dark-haired, dark-eyed, vivacious and extremely attractive, had taken a week off from her job buying and selling stamps to come for a holiday in Ibiza. She met Paco and François, and never went home. Middle-class and convent-educated, she had no particular interest in Buddhism, but she certainly liked the people who practised it. 'They were so calm and peaceful, good to be around,' she said. In particular she liked Paco. Their relationship was soon established.

Their easygoing island existence lost much of its appeal when Lama Yeshe arrived in 1977 to teach a two-week course there. Maria had never met anyone like him. 'We'd had some teachings from some more traditional lamas who had come with Lama Yeshe, and although I had an open mind I thought all the adoration, the prostrations before them a bit too much. Then Lama Yeshe came. More than twice the number of people turned up to see him – the excitement level was very high. He came in smiling at everyone, looking so kind. Then he started to laugh. He kept on laughing, laughing.

'I'd never seen anyone like him. His energy, the power coming out of him, was incredible. He was transmitting with his face, hands, his whole body – every way he could to make us understand. I didn't understand a word he said but something happened inside me. I can't describe the feeling, but it was very strong. Spontaneously I put my hands together. I knew this was a man I could dedicate my life to,' she said.

And so Maria, Paco and François approached Lama Yeshe with the idea of starting a retreat centre on mainland Spain. Lama listened to their plans and agreed. Ibiza was good for initiating interest in Buddhism, but somewhere more 'serious' was needed to consolidate the practice. Lama contributed his own suggestion – the retreat centre should be open to people of all religions who wanted time, space and peace to develop their interior life. After a long, arduous search they finally found the right spot, a plot of land on top of Spain's highest mountain, Mulhacén, 530 feet above sea level, in the Alpujarra mountains, south of Granada. The air was pure, the view sensational, there was no noise, no disturbance from man or machine. It was also totally remote and inaccessible. For six years Paco and François put all their energy and money into making it habitable, building not only the retreat cabins and meditation house but also the road leading to it – by hand. It was a Herculean task, a creation inspired by their devotion.

Their efforts were rewarded by the sudden, unsolicited arrival of His Holiness, the Dalai Lama, who went first to Bubión, where he made a point of meeting the local priest and celebrating Mass with him, and then to the retreat centre which he named 'Osel-Ling' ('Place of Clear Light'), meaning the clear light of the purest, most subtle mind, the final goal of meditation. No one was quite sure what had prompted the Dalai Lama to make this curious detour from his busy European tour to visit a remote Buddhist outpost run by keen, but utterly unimportant Buddhist students.

Later, when Paco, inspired by the light he had seen in his son's face, came up with the name Osel, Maria initially hesitated. It seemed pretentious, too much to live up to. Here François stepped in. 'You have put so much into the centre, it's right the centre should now be part of you,' he reasoned. Maria relented.

While Paco had physically made the centre she had physically made the children, living across the mountain in Bubión where amenities were more suitable for bringing up babies. Her union with Paco had been remarkably fertile, much to her own alarm. She had never wanted children, her maternal instinct not being at all strong, and her desire for independence enormous. She complained loudly to Lama Yeshe – bemoaning the fact that she wasn't free to engage in long spiritual retreats like her unattached friends. 'Your children are your retreat,' he answered. 'You should relate to each one of them as though they were Buddha, because you never know who they are. Even if they are not Buddha it is good for your mind to think like that. Besides, it is true that everyone has the potential to become Buddha, and so it is good for the children for you to treat them that way,' he told her.

Nevertheless, when Osel was conceived she was furious. She had four children under six: Yeshe, five years old, Harmonia four, Lobsang two and Dolma only five months. She was alone most of the time with the children (Paco being busy at the centre) in an overcrowded small house, with no help and large financial worries. A new child was just what she didn't want. Ironically a few weeks previously Paco had tried to persuade her to have an IUD fitted – the other methods of contraception having singularly failed – but the idea was repugnant to her. She'd been to the doctor but had come away knowing she could not go through with it. Lama Yeshe had just died and Maria, trying to think of some way to appease Paco, said to him, 'Well, maybe Lama Yeshe is looking for a mother.' Paco was not convinced. Three weeks later she discovered she was pregnant yet again (in spite of their usual contraceptive methods) and as she ranted at Paco, he acidly threw her joke back at her. 'Maybe it's Lama,' he sarcastically retorted.

The thought that maybe it could be Lama inside her was, however, the only thing that kept Maria from total despair. 'It was a fantasy, the only thing that gave me energy to cope. I never believed it for a second,' she said.

At this point all the FPMT centres around the world got a letter from Lama Zopa saying there was no need for the students to continue to pray for the quick return of Lama Yeshe since a woman was already pregnant with him. Maria and Paco received the news with mixed feelings. On the one hand they were delighted at the thought that they might see their beloved Lama again. On the other they were naturally dubious about the whole issue of reincarnation. They had the intellectual knowledge, like so many of us, but no personal experience. On balance they considered this a golden opportunity to see how it worked. They didn't realize how close they were going to get.

Maria had well and truly dropped her fantasy about Osel being Lama Yeshe after he was born. She was far too busy with all her domestic chores to indulge in such day-dreams. She did notice, however, that Osel continued to be a 'different' child. He didn't seem to need to be with her, or his siblings. He was very self-contained, almost meditative, and could spend long hours contemplating unlikely things. 'He used to hold and look at subtle things, like a single hair, for a long time. Most children don't have the physical ability, nor the interest in such things,' mused Maria. 'He had strong powers of concentration, too.'

When Osel was five months old, Paco and Maria took him to Switzerland in a small basket for the Kalachakra initiations being given by the Dalai Lama, and later went to Germany to attend the FPMT meetings, now being presided over by Lama Zopa, who had succeeded Lama Yeshe as head of this rapidly growing organization. When Lama Zopa spotted the baby he asked his name and when told 'Osel, from Osel-Ling', he burst out laughing. Later, during a ceremony he was giving, he cryptically remarked, 'Lama is very close to us at this moment. He might even be in the room with us.' Maria spotted a pregnant woman in the audience and wondered. Or was Lama Zopa referring to the spiritual presence of Lama Yeshe which was close at this time? No one thought he was talking about the little figure in the basket.

Two months later Lama Zopa came to Osel Ling to give a course. During a tea-break Maria left the meditation room and on her return found, somewhat to her astonishment, that Lama Zopa had lifted Osel on to the throne with him and her child was busy playing with the dorje and bell – ritual implements used by Tibetan lamas. That lunchtime Lama Zopa summoned Maria to him and questioned her thoroughly about Osel's conception, and several other issues. He didn't pass any comment. Instead, just before he left, he held a long-life ceremony for Osel, explaining to the parents: 'Osel is a very special child. He has the karma to benefit many, many sentient beings in this life. Thousands maybe. Look after him well. Don't put him in any polluted place. Don't let people smoke near him. Take great, great care of him.' Then he gave Maria Lama Yeshe's mala (rosary), the one he'd had with him when he died. Maria was nervous. Had she influenced Lama Zopa in some way by her crazy fantasies while she was pregnant? Had Lama Zopa somehow picked up her thoughts and been subconsciously directed by them?

But then life continued in its domestic humdrum way and Maria, surrounded by five small children, pushed the things Lama Zopa had said to the back of her mind.

10

THE SEARCH

Meanwhile Lama Zopa had been conducting his own extremely diligent search over the past few months for the rebirth of his precious guru who he was sure would honour his promise to return again to this earth to continue his great work of guiding sentient beings out of the wheel of uncontrolled birth and death.

In accordance with Tibetan tradition, which has its own precise procedure for tracking down reincarnated lamas, he'd consulted various oracles. There had been a variety of pointers. One had indicated a western child born to a couple of Lama Yeshe's students living in Kopan itself. Another had actually predicted that the child would be born in Osel-Ling and that the mother's name was Maria, or the Tibetan equivalent. And a clairvoyant nun, a student of Lama Zopa's, had looked in a mirror and come up with the name Paco and seen the profile of the mother. At the time it had meant nothing to her. Lama Zopa took note, but not too much notice. He said oracles were not always reliable and much stronger proof was required in this case.

He paid attention to his dreams. One poignantly vivid one revealed Lama Yeshe declaring that he was about to take another human form. He'd heard the cries of his students calling out to him in need and suffering, and could no longer stay in the realm of bliss, ignoring their plight. A later dream showed him a small child with bright, penetrating eyes, crawling on the floor of a meditation room. He was male and a westerner.

So Lama Zopa, in his new role as successor to Lama Yeshe and head of the rapidly growing FPMT, travelled around the world visiting the various centres, giving teachings, guiding meditations, endowing initiations – and keeping a watchful eye for any baby who, to his clairvoyant mind, was in any way 'special'.

When he came to Osel-Ling in the autumn of 1985 he saw Osel

crawling on the Gompa floor. He had clear far-seeing eyes. He was a westerner. His face was exactly the same as the child in his dream. Lama Zopa sat up. He brought Osel on to the throne with him to have a closer look. Yes, it was definitely the child of his dream. He noted the child's familiarity and liking for the dorje and bell. That could have been a coincidence. More subtly he recognized that Osel was leaning against him in a similar manner to Lama Yeshe when he was paralysed with a stroke in California just before he died. He also watched the way Osel rubbed his head round and round, a habit Lama Yeshe always had.

Interested he called Maria to him. When had Osel been conceived? Maria thought back. It was the exact date when Lama Zopa had had his first dream of Lama Yeshe announcing he was going to be reborn. He asked Maria if she had had any notable dreams during that time. She replied that one had in fact stuck in her mind. She had been in a large cathedral where Lama Yeshe was giving teachings to a huge crowd. Many were Christians and they were all kneeling rather than sitting cross-legged on the floor. With everyone else she went up to Lama to receive his blessing and when he touched her she felt as though water, blissful golden-white water was pouring though her, purifying her. Lama Zopa made no comment.

He asked when was the last time she had seen Lama Yeshe and whether he had said anything significant to her. Maria remembered the occasion well. It was a full year before he died, in February 1983. Lama had come to Spain, and she, Paco and François had gone to him with practical questions about running the retreat centre. He had given nothing other than advice on Osel-Ling, because this was all they had talked about. But Lama Zopa could hear for himself what had been said since they had videoed the meeting for future reference. Lama Zopa replied that he'd very much like to see it.

Watching the video, he was struck by some fairly incongruous remarks Lama Yeshe had made in the context of giving practical advice. At one point he had said, 'Osel-Ling is such a beautiful place. It reminds me very much of the Himalayas. At some point in the future I'd like to spend a lot of time there.' More significantly he'd remarked to Maria and Paco, 'I know how much you have done for the centre, how dedicated you have been. I shall never forget you.

Even if I die I will never forget you. We have much business, much karma business between us.' At the time the words had meant nothing to Maria and Paco and they had promptly forgotten them. Now Lama Zopa began to glean their true meaning.

In fact Maria and Paco were ideal candidates for the job of parenting a reincarnated Tibetan lama – with all the demands and controversy it would inevitably bring. They were both down-to-earth, no-nonsense, stable, hard-working, honest people. They already had a large family and so a fifth child who would be separated from them for long periods of time would not be the same wrench as if it were happening with an only child. More importantly, Maria was not a clinging mother. Quite the opposite. While she conscientiously looked after her children, she could quite happily let them go. Maria had openly stated to Lama Yeshe several times that she did not need children to fulfil her life. It was an ideal quality for a son who needed to get on with his mission in life, unhampered by maternal possessiveness. And then there was Paco – steady, strong, gentle, utterly devoted to the Buddhist path, and with a natural affinity for children, a quality that was to come in very useful.

The case for Osel Hita Torres was growing. At this point Lama Zopa wrote to His Holiness, the Dalai Lama, who all the time had been doing his own prayers and observations for the rebirth of Lama Yeshe, with a list of possible candidates, who Lama Zopa had observed and who all showed some favourable signs. There were ten children in all, including, amongst others, three Tibetans from Nepal; two children from Tibet who were born near the area where Lama Yeshe's family lived and two western children, one with an Indian father and western mother. After a while the Dalai Lama replied that he had meditated on the names and one of them definitely was Lama Yeshe's reincarnation, but he wanted more time to make sure. Two months later the Dalai Lama contacted Lama Zopa again and said that the name that repeatedly came up was Osel's. The evidence now seemed conclusive. Lama Zopa's own convictions had been ratified by the person whom he, and 14 million other Buddhists consider the most holy being on earth, a living Buddha, His Holiness, the Dalai Lama.

The call came at breakfast time on 18 April 1986. Maria, surrounded by the chaos and noise of her large family squabbling over the cereal packets, could hardly hear the soft voice of Lama Zopa calling from India. Would she please come to Delhi *next week* and bring Osel with her for some tests? The money could be acquired from the resident Geshe at the retreat centre who happened to be holding on to the exact amount for some unspecified purpose. Maria could hardly take it in. What was Lama Zopa intimating? Was Osel going to be tested along with other children to see if he was, after all, Lama Yeshe? With her mind in a complete whirl and the rush to get ready, she hardly had time to think about the ramifications of her journey.

Their arrival in Delhi hardly seemed auspicious. The pre-monsoon heat was suffocating and Osel, used to the fresh, spring air of the high Spanish mountains, began to wane visibly. He was jet-lagged into the bargain. The quarters they were living in were crowded. He got horribly bitten by mosquitoes, and then he fell down, cutting his eye.

Maria didn't feel too good either. She was anxious about what was happening (still harbouring guilt feelings about the part her sub-conscious thoughts might have played in the matter) and her 14-month-old son was fractious. Then she was told the reason they had come to Delhi was that the Dalai Lama was there and wanted to see Osel before he went overseas. They got ready: Lama Zopa; his secretary Jacie Keeley; Yeshe Khadro, the Australian nun; Maria and Osel. Bouquets of flowers were bought (Yeshe Khadro purchased a solitary white rose for Osel to give) and traditional white scarves by way of offerings.

At the appointed hour they were duly ushered into the hotel room where he was staying, the traditional scarves were offered and the bouquets of flowers were piled on a nearby table. The Dalai Lama took a long look at Osel and kindly took him up into his arms. Osel's face was transformed into a picture of pure rapture. He wriggled to get down and ran over to the table where, amongst the pile of flowers, he found his one white rose, pulled it free, ran back to the Dalai Lama again and gently hit him on the cheek with it. The Dalai Lama laughed in delight. The others were amazed. No one had told Osel that the white rose was his gift, and certainly no one had prompted his spontaneous act. The Dalai Lama looked at Maria and told her that Osel would give further evidence of who he was when he got older.

Still nothing definite had been said. Instead Lama Zopa announced that they were all going to get into cars and drive some 250 miles to Dharamsala. They drove for 15 hours non-stop, Osel becoming increasingly testy. Maria had no idea what was going on. Unbeknown to her, the Dalai Lama had counselled Lama Zopa that announcing Osel's identity at this stage might be courting problems. Fourteen months was an exceptionally young age to recognize a reincarnated lama, most tulkus being officially instated at four or five years old. Lama Zopa was in a dilemma. Nothing on earth would induce him to bring trouble to his beloved Lama's life, yet he knew how badly his western students needed not only the proof of reincarnation, but the living presence of Lama Yeshe in their midst once more. On that long car journey to Dharamsala he was meditating on the right course of action.

When they arrived his mind was made up. He called several of Lama Yeshe's students, monks and nuns who were studying or retreating at the Tushita Centre, dressed Osel in one of his own yellow shirts, placed him on Lama Yeshe's throne in Lama Yeshe's room, did three prostrations before him and gave him a mandala offering.

'Here is your guru,' he said.

With that, Osel, who until then had been beyond exhaustion, flopped back against the cushions and threw aside his bottle, suddenly fired with energy. His whole demeanour changed. He sat bolt upright, wide awake, eyes shining, his face full of vitality. He picked up the dorje and bell in his small hands, the correct hands, and with tremendous gusto waved them in the air as a Tibetan lama should. He put them down and repeated the action again, and again. Seven or eight times. And all the time laughing, laughing. People began to cry. It was so like Lama. He had come back to them. Maria felt paralysed inside. Finally she understood. The child she had carried and borne was being hailed as the reincarnation of the great Lama Yeshe – the man who had shown such extraordinary skill and dedication in guiding westerners to Enlightenment. How could this be?

Later she spoke to Lama Zopa. Why hadn't he warned her beforehand? He replied he had to be completely sure and then asked if she believed. 'I don't know. It's difficult. I think I want more proof,' she answered honestly.

More proof was forthcoming. Osel still had to undertake the

traditional tests, given to all reincarnate lamas. And so, as Tibetans have done for hundreds of years, Lama Zopa sought out some of Lama Yeshe's possessions, mixed them with others of similar type, and asked Osel to pick out those that were rightfully his. He started with a mala (rosary), a fairly ordinary wooden beaded one, a favourite of Lama's, which he placed on a low table along with four others almost identical in style and one made out of bright crystal beads which he thought would act as a natural red-herring to a baby of 14 months.

Then, with Maria and a few western disciples as witnesses, he commanded Osel, 'Give me your mala from your past life.' Osel turned his head away as if bored. Then he whipped it back again and without hesitation went straight for the correct mala, which he grabbed with both hands, raising it above his head, grinning, in a triumphant victory salute. An Australian monk, Max Redlich, was ready with two cameras, a brand-new one and an antique device belonging to Lama Yeshe. 'Use the old one,' charged Lama Zopa. Max ignored him, reaching for the sophisticated camera instead. It jammed. Max missed the shot.

After a break Lama Zopa set up the bells – there were eight of them. This time Osel dallied. He picked up the bells in pairs, ringing them and setting them down. Lama Zopa instructed again, 'Give me your bell from your past life.' Maria, watching the spectacle, never believed her child could perform the same miracle twice. He was so young. Such a feat must surely be beyond him. Osel continued to play with all the bells, picking them up and putting them down again. To the onlookers it looked as if he were teasing them all. Lama Zopa repeated the instruction. 'Osel, give me *your* bell.' Osel delicately, but with great determination, picked up Lama Zopa's hand and put it on the correct bell. This time Max was ready with the functioning camera.

Osel had passed the tests and could now be formally recognized as the legitimate incarnation of the late Lama Thubten Yeshe. The western monks, nuns and disciples in Dharamsala, who had all been intimately acquainted with Lama Yeshe, could not take their eyes off the fair-haired toddler running in their midst in nappies. Here again, they were told, was their great guru – but in such a different form. For most, it was hard to accept totally. They watched, looking for yet more signs. Osel gave them.

At the top of the mountain, above the Tushita Retreat Centre, is the house where the great Kyabje Ling Rinpoche, senior tutor to the Dalai Lama, and 97th Throneholder of Je Tsong Khapa, once lived. He passed away in December 1983 and in tribute to this eminent scholar and spiritual master the Dalai Lama decreed that his body be preserved according to the ancient Tibetan method. It exists to this day, placed in the drawing room of this rather unremarkable colonial house, sitting in the lotus position, the hands in the mudras (symbolic stylized gestures) of giving teachings and with a look of utter serenity on the ancient, wise, and consummately compassionate face.

Osel was taken up there with Maria and Max Redlich. When he saw the figure he threw himself on the ground in a full prostration. He got up and did it again. Three times. Maria and Max were astonished. Where had he learnt such things? There was more to come. Later he came across the Stupa dedicated to his former root guru Trijang Rinpoche. Without prompting, Osel set off at a trot around the Stupa, circumnambulating it in a clockwise direction as every good Tibetan pilgrim should. He stopped occasionally to do prostrations, and to make sure that the others were following and doing likewise. For a 14-month-old child his behaviour was extraordinary, to say the least.

Perhaps the most touching scene of all was when Osel was taken to meet the reincarnation of Trijang Rinpoche, a four-year-old with a commanding presence, and a wisdom far beyond his years, who was already receiving hundreds of Tibetans for blessing. Lama Yeshe had been devoted to his great teacher, and had wept openly when he died, saying that everything he had been able to do had come from the kindness of Trijang Rinpoche. Now Osel was told who he was going to meet. The child could hardly contain himself – his whole body shook with excitement. Bearing gifts, they drove to the new Trijang Rinpoche's house – Osel still quivering with anticipation – and there the two tiny figures met, beaming at each other with obvious delight. Osel then reached for some money that was meant as an offering and with great joy handed it over to Trijang Rinpoche who, with equal delight, handed it back again. This exchange went on for several minutes, the two participants clearly enjoying their game enormously. When Osel left he was walking on tiptoe, his feet hardly touching the ground.

Those who were witness to Osel's behaviour watched in wonder. They talked among themselves, musing on the strangeness of this small child who had suddenly come among them. And so word rapidly spread about the extraordinary phenomenon of the baby Spanish lama.

11

BUBIÓN

After that initial, rather disconcerting encounter in London I travelled to Bubión to see Osel in his home territory. Ostensibly the pretext was to write a story, but as so often my journalism was also serving to quench a driving personal curiosity. Instinct told me that this was a marvellous story, but my own bond with Lama Yeshe added an extra, vital dimension.

It was just before Christmas when photographer Terry Fincher (whom I had worked with on several Fleet Street assignments) and I made the three-hour car journey from Malaga airport through the nasty concrete jungle of the Costa del Sol and up the winding mountain road to Bubión. The Alpujarra mountains were experiencing a late, glorious autumn, the russet and gold of the leaves outlined starkly against a bright blue sky. The higher we climbed the more enchanting southern Spain became – the utilitarian boxes of the coast giving way to the genuine Moorish architecture of the region. Terry became more excited. This was perfect country for photographs.

We found Bubión just before sunset, clinging perilously to the highest reaches of the mountain, just below the snowline. It was charming, but nothing much – just a main road running through a cluster of houses, all white-washed, built in the traditional manner with small balconies and bougainvillea climbing the walls, and the animals housed in the downstairs room. There was a village school, a couple of shops, a village square, the parish church and the new addition – a modern hotel which Paco had helped to build, to cater for the growing summer tourist trade. Now, thankfully, there were only the residents, farmers mostly, eking a modest living out of their crops and livestock, and a surprisingly large group of foreign artists and writers, drawn there by the natural beauty and the simplicity of the life.

It was crisp when we got out of the car and the aromatic smell of wood smoke filled the air. As I watched the donkeys, mules and cows being herded into their stables beneath the houses and heard the church bells of St Sebastian ring out, I couldn't help but recall another story, nearly 2,000 years old, of a child born among animals, whose mother's name was Maria and whose father was a carpenter and whose entry into the world caused both joy and controversy.

We found Maria with four of her children in her house – a stone 'two-up, two-down' with flagstone floor, wooden beams and a large open fire roaring in a corner of the downstairs living room. Osel was aready living, we were told, in the retreat centre on the mountain opposite with Paco, the resident Tibetan Geshe, his translator, a handful of monks and nuns, and the retreators. Instinctively I reacted. Was this right? Osel was just 22 months old. All the modern western psychological theories (expounded in angst by my many working-mother friends, that a child needed to be with his mother for at least the first five years of his life if he were to be emotionally secure) sprung to mind. And again that burning issue of conditioning. Was Osel going to be allowed to be anything *but* a Tibetan lama?

Maria smiled, saying Osel was perfectly happy; he often came down to spend time with the whole family, and besides Lama Zopa had said it was better for him to spend his time in the peaceful, spiritual atmosphere of a meditation centre.

Over the following three days I saw a lot of Osel, while I interviewed and scrutinized for signs of Lama Yeshe, and Terry took a battery of evocative photographs in that perfect setting. Playing with his brothers and sisters at home, climbing the wood-pile outside his house, he could have passed for any other child – apart from his maroon skirts flapping around his legs and his hair cropped uncommonly short. But it was at the retreat centre, Osel-Ling, that his 'difference' stood out.

Arriving the first morning at dawn, having climbed the last four miles with the wheels of the jeep hanging over the mountain edge, I watched the orange sun rise, the mists swirling in the valleys below, the high majestic peaks ascending into the clear blue sky and, with that awesome hush that seems to permeate holy places, I was instantly transported back to Kopan. I drew in my breath.

The similarity was uncanny. The little retreat huts dotted about the mountainside, the Tibetan teacher, the assembly of red and gold robes, that atmosphere of peace and sanity that comes from people devoting time to looking within for the truth, even the Tibetan dogs scampering about, all conjured up that rarefied atmosphere of the Himalayan kingdom.

Osel was apparently perfectly at home. He lived with his father in one simple room attached to the main building which contained at one end a low altar, and at the other a small heap of toys. They were clearly very close – the male bond truly established. Paco, with his gentle, patient nature, was admirably equipped to deal with the demands of a small child. Not only that, it occurred to me later that Osel was already being prepared for the predominantly male community of the monastery he was to find himself in. He had, said his parents, a natural affinity with the Geshe, and indeed any Tibetan lamas he met, seeking them out, preferring their company to anybody else's. He would spend hours with them. I had seen this for myself in London. Osel had only just met Geshe Wangchen but he would toddle into his room, ignoring his family and the westerners present, spending hours in there with him. And no, said Paco, he hadn't cried for his mother once. He simply didn't seem to miss her. Of course he enjoyed his days at Bubión with Maria and the rest of the family, but he never minded leaving, and seemed pleased to get back into the jeep to return to Osel-Ling.

On that first morning I had breakfast with the community and watched with some relief when Osel threw his porridge across the table like any normal child his age. And he was told off for it, too. One didn't like to stare but it was hard not to. How does a baby Rinpoche behave? What thoughts go through his head? How much of him is infant, how much transcendental wisdom? I tried to behave normally, as I would with any child, and as I relaxed Osel looked straight at me across the table and wrinkled up his nose and eyes in an exact replica expression of Lama Yeshe. It was deliberate, exact, unnerving. This child had the same sense of mischief, an adult sense of humour, and he seemed to be, well, pulling my leg!

This pattern was to repeat itself often. When the expectation for some sign as to his holiness was there, Osel would perversely do nothing, or behave singularly badly. When you were completely yourself and genuinely open to him he would do something that would absolutely stagger you. Whatever was going on, he seemed to be utterly in control of it.

And as I'd first seen in London, Osel was clearly a very contented child, surprisingly self-contained and with an energy that was literally irrepressible. Like Lama. His physicality was enormous. Like Lama. Here was no vapid, ethereal 'spirit-child', looking as though he belonged to another, finer, dimension. Osel was very much of this earth – sturdy, strong, planting his feet firmly on the ground as he walked, or rather, ran. Like Lama. Osel was solid, completely at home in his body, confident with every gesture and move he made.

In fact he seemed to be completely without fear. I watched his favourite game – hurling himself off the flat roof of the meditation room, squealing with glee, totally trusting that somehow Paco's arms would be there to catch him. That done, he'd run off down the steep rocky mountainside, sure-footed as a goat (or yak) while anxious adults pounded after him, slipping on the loose stones, terrified that their new-found guru would disappear over the precipice and be lost in the abyss below. Osel was not faint-hearted! On the contrary he was showing signs of being larger than life. Just like Lama.

He was also an extrovert. He reached out to people at every opportunity, in his own baby way, wanting to make contact. And this in spite of his natural self-containment. But there was something else, something indefinable. It was a charisma, a presence. It was partly to do with his effervescent energy (a well-spring of joy you felt was gurgling away inside him), partly to do with the fact that he was clearly in control of everything, in a strange adult way, and yet something else again. You felt as though there was something special about him. While writing this and musing on Osel's strange quality I came across some mystic writings given by the Archangel Michael to a medium in Glastonbury, England, in a book called *The Winds of Truth*, which had been donated to the Kopan Library by Lama Yeshe himself.

'You have a saying "odd man out",' said the book. 'These odd men and women in families are born to the Earth Planet for a definite purpose, not in their case of necessity in connection with karma, but for the fulfilment of some Great Work. There is an "apartness" about such children, a silence, a deep thoughtfulness. They *know* they are "different"; they are aware of their "oddness". Can these little ones be, in any way, said to *belong* to their parents? No!'

That approached the feeling I experienced with Osel. Not that he was all sweetness and light! At the end of the second day, as Terry was trying to coax him into one more shot, Osel turned round and kicked him in the shins. What was this? A bad-tempered Buddha? I was shocked, disappointed even. I went away and thought about it. It was perfectly natural behaviour. Osel was tired, and had been co-operating with the camera for two full days. Maybe a 22-month-old child, no matter how saintly, has only one real way of saying when enough is enough.

But the imperfection, no matter how trivial, was magnified when held up against the ideal I was carrying in my mind. It would always be like this, I realized. He could never pick his nose, be grumpy, or unco-operative without sceptical witnesses judging him to be a 'fake'. And yet surely if any divine being did incarnate on this earth, woud they not also take on the limitations of a physical body, including tiredness, sickness, and sometimes an irritated nervous system? If the divine were purely divine and not mixed with the human, would we recognize it at all? And hadn't all the saints demonstrated human failings at times?

Then came the sweetness. I watched him say grace before lunch, putting his hands together and saying the Buddhist mantra 'Om Ah Hum' over the plate of food before him. I followed him into the meditation room, saw him sit down on a cushion cross-legged as though, for all the world, that was where he belonged, rocking back and forth as any lama would do while caught in the deep concentration of profound meditation. He cuddled a puppy and took the venerable grey-haired Geshe for a walk, two figures walking along a mountain path, both dressed alike, one tiny and young, one large and old, holding hands, perfectly at ease in each other's company. At one stage, apropos of nothing, he came across to where I was sitting, put his hand into mine and smiled straight into my eyes. A nun looking on remarked that it made exactly the same picture as the photograph taken of Lama Yeshe and me on the path in Kopan the last time I saw him, after that stupendous talk on compassion.

To me, Osel was magnetic – a new experience for someone who had never been drawn to any child under 16 for more than a few minutes. Whenever I looked at him I wanted to smile. He was solemn and yet funny at the same time. He was precocious, certainly, but not spoilt. He was a magic child.

Back in Bubión I talked to Maria, who was learning English especially to deal with the barrage of questions being directed at her by the press, and who was more gregarious by nature than her husband, about how she now felt about her youngest son, the difference he had made to their lives, and any evidence she had gathered about him being Lama Yeshe.

'At first, after Dharamsala, it was difficult,' she confided. 'How could I equate my feelings as a mother with my feelings for my guru? I wasn't sure how I should behave with Osel. If he's naughty, should I scold him? I turned to Lama Zopa for advice and he gave me practical guidelines to follow, which have helped. He said he was to be corrected when he misbehaved, like any other child! And I still do get angry with him. There have been some difficult moments for me – like when he is with other people and I want him to be good, and act like Lama, and he doesn't! If I push him it just becomes worse. I've realized that I must relax, and allow him to be himself. He's so sensitive, he soaks up whatever atmosphere he is in, like a sponge. When people feel for him like Lama Yeshe, that's what he gives back. When they treat him like a baby that is how he behaves. He seems to tune in to people and mirrors back what they are feeling.

'My Buddhist training has helped. We are taught that everyone who comes into this world has their own identity and the mother and father only provide the body and the care. The parents are not responsible for who that child is,' she said.

By this time Maria had had time to get used to the idea that her son was a reincarnate lama and had come to believe it, as had the rest of the family. 'I now have no doubts. I truly believe my son is Lama Yeshe,' she said simply. There had, she said, been plenty of proof.

'On an everyday level – small things, like the fact that he loves Tibetan tea, ever since Lama Zopa gave it to him in Dharamsala, and all Tibetan food. None of my other children like it – in fact, they hate it,' Maria told me. I was not surprised. Tibetan tea made out of salted butter is definitely an acquired taste! It is repellent. Yet Osel gulps it down with the thirst of a dying man. The typical Tibetan fare of tsampa, mo-mos and tugpa would hardly tickle the palate of a normal western infant either. 'Osel eats his fruit strangely, too – like Lama Yeshe. He sucks out the pulp and throws the rest away.'

There has been other behaviour which has made her and other people sit up. Shortly after she and Osel returned from Dharamsala, when Osel was 15 months old, Maria invited her parents to stay. Her mother, in particular, was extremely worried and sceptical about the whole issue of her grandson being declared the reincarnation of a Tibetan lama. During their stay they played a video of the Dalai Lama's visit to Spain, an amateur production, inconsistent in quality and over two hours long.

'Osel sat in front of the screen the whole way through, putting his hands together and blowing kisses at the Dalai Lama whenever he appeared. It was remarkable. No child of his age is able to sit through *any* film for two hours – even if it were Walt Disney. Yet Osel was transfixed. He didn't move. His delight at seeing the Dalai Lama, and his adoration was tremendous. After that, my mother believed,' said Maria.

Curiously, the local people greeted the news of Osel's identity with surprising equanimity. 'They are simple people, primitive, belonging to the earth and animals. They have very good hearts. When they heard about Osel they came to the house congratulating me, bringing flowers. They are proud to have him in the village. To them he is going to be a new kind of Pope. A shopkeeper said to me, "Well, we have never seen God, so why shouldn't we accept this?" It is only the intellectuals who like to question,' she said. And one wonders how much ground the Dalai Lama himself prepared for this unusual event when he made that impromptu visit to Bubión and the parish priest, long before Osel was born.

Life had changed dramatically for the Hita Torres family in the past few months. With a child rapidly reaching celebrity status, Maria and Paco had learnt to deal with the hordes of international press, and television camera crews wending their way to the tiny village of Bubión to record the advent of Osel. Paco admitted he found the whole thing overwhelming, but Maria was clearly taking it in her stride. 'It is how Lama would have wanted it. He was always encouraging us to "think big" and he, himself, was not at all afraid of the media,' she said.

Maria and Paco had begun their international, jet-setting life. Osel was merely continuing his. When news spread that Lama Yeshe's rebirth had been discovered, invitations began pouring into the Bubión household from Lama Yeshe's students scattered across the world, asking them to come and visit. Already they'd been to Europe and the USA, and further tours were in the pipeline. It was on these trips that Osel gave further evidence that he was a special child.

In France he had come face to face with his first life-size statue of the Buddha. He approached the Buddha and began behaving with him as though he were an old friend. 'It was as if they had a good relationship. Osel put his hand in his, and stood there with him, quite happy. It was something quite different to see,' explained Maria.

In Holland he'd demonstrated yet again that perverse ability to direct his will precisely where he wanted, and not perform to others' expectations. Maria described it: 'There were a lot of students around him, wanting to get near, seeking his attention, needing a lot of things from him. Osel wasn't too interested. Instead he saw a woman alone in the garden. He went outside, went straight up to her, opened her handbag and found there the katag (white scarf) that she had brought to offer him, but was obviously too shy to present. He allowed the woman to give it to him – she was so thrilled. I didn't know how he knew such a thing. He couldn't have picked that up from anybody.'

In America Osel proved himself to be very much at home – just like Lama Yeshe. At one house they visited, where Lama often used to stay, Osel ran through the front door and headed straight for the room which was Lama Yeshe's. He bounced up and down on the bed and then, much to the onlookers' further amazement, found the key to the cupboard Lama Yeshe always used to use, hidden in a drawer where it was always kept. Perhaps his *pièce de résistance*, however, was his behaviour with Geshe Sopa, at Madison. Geshe Sopa used to be Lama Yeshe's teacher back in Tibet, and Lama always confessed he was rather nervous of this kindly but brilliantly clever man who exacted such high standards in both studies and discipline from his young monks. 'Osel walked

into Geshe Sopa's room and straight away did a full-length prostration before him. He got up, and did it again. Even Lama Zopa,
and the other Tibetan lamas present were taken aback at this. Osel
wasn't prompted to do a prostration – no one had done one before
him. It was absolutely spontaneous. Where does he learn such
things – if not from a previous life? He is so young to be behaving
like this,' Maria said.

In California those who had watched Lama Yeshe die greeted
his return with a mixture of joy and bemusement. As the car
bearing Osel drove through the giant redwoods of the beautiful
Vajrapani Centre they saw the fair, indubitably western baby-face
of the child who had been hailed as the new Lama Yeshe at the
window. No one spoke. The atmosphere as Osel got out of the car
was pregnant with meaning. This was the place where the body of
Lama Yeshe had lain in the open coffin, emanating sweet odours.
This was the place where he had been ritually cremated. This was
the place where, as the funeral flames roared, a rainbow had
appeared in the sky for all to see, even though it was a brilliant
blue day with not a drop of rain.

Osel's eyes didn't fall on any one of those brave people who had
nursed him until death; he was mesmerized by the small but
beautiful Stupa erected to Lama Yeshe's memory standing before
him. As he got out of the car he ran towards it, eyes shining with
pleasure, as if to say, 'What a wonderful Stupa you made me.'
Those who watched had the unusual experience of witnessing
a small child examine the death memorial they'd erected to
his predecessor. For the average western psyche this was a lot to
take in!

Later they held a religious ceremony for him, to welcome him
home, so to speak. At the high point, a mandala (a pyramid of
grain and coloured beads, built up on a silver dish over three tiers,
and representing the universe) is offered to the guru. Osel, in the
place of honour, solemnly took a small coloured bead from the
mandala and walked along the front row of disciples, placing
the bead on the crown of each, as a blessing. That done, he calmly
went back to the mandala and replaced the bead carefully. Again
he acted completely spontaneously. Maria claimed no one had
taught him to do this – and indeed he'd never done it before. 'Even
to hold a bead and place it on the head of a row of people is quite

difficult for a child of his age – as to putting it back again, most children would just fling it aside! For a 20-month-old child his actions were extraordinary,' she said.

He had performed a similar act when he was even younger, continued Maria. They'd been conducting a small meeting in the meditation room at Osel-Ling, and there was some dispute amongst them. Osel, sitting on a meditation cushion, listening to the disagreement, suddenly got up, walked over to the altar, took down a small statue of Shakyamuni Buddha and calmly went round placing it on the heads of everyone present. Suddenly there was no argument!

This was particularly strange because, until a couple of months before, Osel had been exposed to very few, if any, religious objects. At home, in Bubión, Maria was not one for having altars and statues of the Buddha around. 'I have never liked that kind of thing. The respect is there, but I prefer it to be on the inside. And for me, guru devotion has always meant trying to put the teachings into practice,' she said, honestly. 'How Osel became so familiar with statues and the ritual in such a short space of time is a complete mystery to me.'

But still the issue of conditioning remained. I tackled her about it. Did she not think that the life Osel was now leading, separated from the rest of the family, in the rarefied environment of a retreat centre, with all the attention he was receiving from ex-Lama Yeshe disciples, was contriving to make him into a spiritual master, whether he was or not?

Maria thought for a moment and replied: 'From my experience with children it is not possible to *make* them what they are not. It is not possible – especially at this age. You cannot make a 20-month-old child do anything he does not want to do. And none of my other children, no matter how intelligent, would have been able to do the things Osel has done. It isn't in them. Besides, he is not locked up. He is free. When he travels he does so in ordinary clothes (and talks to everyone as he goes!) and meets lots of non-Buddhist people. He knows my family. We do not push him. My mother asks, what will happen if he turns out not to be a lama? I reply that I don't care. I personally do not mind whether he is a lama or not. In the future there will be plenty of opportunity for him to choose.

'At the moment we believe what Lama Zopa and the Dalai Lama tell us, and we follow their directions, because we trust them. We've put him in Osel-Ling because Lama Zopa says it's better for him there, and actually he does eat and sleep better when he's there. The noise and confusion of the other children seem to disturb him. In this regard I suppose we are conditioning Osel, but then every parent conditions their child to a certain extent. If you see your child has a propensity to become a doctor or lawyer, the parent will normally try to arrange the education and opportunities for this to be developed. We are only doing that.

'But I am making no predictions for the future. I live for the present and trust that whatever happens will be for the best. What I do know is that Lama Zopa will never do anything to harm any of us. And that since Osel was born our lives have become happier and happier.'

Maria's argument seemed irrefutable. I could concede that most parents condition their children either voluntarily or involuntarily but . . . to my mind the proof of Osel's identity would still be far stronger if his accomplishments emerged from a regular western environment and lifestyle.

I left Bubión enriched for having been there and with more material to feed the cerebral cortex. I'd been enchanted by the scenery, welcomed by Maria and Paco, stimulated by our conversations and intrigued again by Osel himself. After that initial meeting in London I was not disappointed by my further investigations. The *Mail on Sunday* published the story on the front cover of *You* magazine, their colour supplement. They sold every copy. And with Terry's excellent photographs the article was syndicated throughout Europe, Scandinavia, Australia, New Zealand, South Africa and the Far East. The world was obviously ripe for the news of the little Spanish lama.

Coincidentally, at the same time the film *Golden Child* was released. It was the tale of a special Tibetan child, an embodiment of the Compassionate Buddha, kidnapped by evil forces and rescued by the black comedian Eddie Murphy. In spite of the tacky Hollywood treatment of the sensitive and profound subject-matter, the film clearly struck a chord. Now, here was Osel, a living 'Golden Child', embodying all the fascination of eastern mysticism but in a western body.

If Osel was indeed Lama Yeshe he was certainly carrying on his work in no mean way – bringing Buddhism to 20th-century urban western man on a vast scale. He was only 22 months old, yet he had already captured the imagination of people across the globe. Whoever this being was, he was undoubtedly extraordinary. But if his fame was growing, so was his responsibility. The onus was on him to grow into the spiritual being the world expected him to be. A heavy burden for such small shoulders.

12

THE STORIES

It wasn't just his parents and Lama Zopa Rinpoche who were being given repeated signs that Osel had, to say the least, a strong affiliation with Tibetan culture in general and the late Lama Yeshe in particular. On his travels around various continents visiting the FPMT centres, with the spotlight of attention and curiosity constantly focused on him, the fair-haired toddler with the commanding presence continued to demonstrate to many that he possessed an uncanny 'memory' of sayings, actions and mannerisms that could only be attributed to Lama Yeshe. These small, subtle 'personal proofs' often provided more convincing evidence of the child's actual identity than the official tests given by Lama Zopa, if only because they struck home – usually with a force that left the witness stunned.

During my own search for the truth of the matter, I eagerly collected these individual stories. I was riveted by what I heard and was utterly convinced as to the sincerity of the speaker, but I also realized, the more I looked and heard, that reincarnation is no simple matter. Its implications are vast; its complexities enormous and far-reaching. But then so is Mind – that uncharted territory for the West, which is the next frontier of science. Discovering inner space seemed to me an infinitely more exciting and worthwhile adventure than sending rockets to the barren wastes of the moon.

Suzanna Parodi's story was particularly poignant and persuasive. This was the girl who had put her sleeping bag next to mine on that first Kopan course in 1976, and lay shaking through the night, racked by the withdrawal symptoms of drug addiction. She had gone on to lead an extremely creative, productive life back in Italy, becoming a successful textile designer, while keeping in regular touch with Lama Yeshe and the Buddhist centres he had set up.

When news reached her that he was ill, Suzanna was naturally distraught. She owed her life to this man. With typical spontaneity she immediately caught a plane to India. As luck would have it, she caught him at Delhi airport, just as he was leaving for California, where he would die. Because of some administrative mix-up there was no wheelchair available to help Lama Yeshe get to the plane, and so two of his disciples were on either side of him, helping him walk. At the sight of her once strong, vital Lama looking so thin and wasted, Suzanna burst into tears.

Lama Yeshe looked at her and smiled. He took his arms from the shoulders that were propping him up, raised them above his head and swung them back and forth, clicking his fingers, as though doing a dance. 'Don't worry my daughter, I am all right,' he said, proving that his great spirit was alive and thriving even if his body wasn't. That was the last she ever saw of him.

Like all of us, Suzanna was agog when she heard that his reincarnation had not only been found but formally announced by Lama Zopa in Dharamsala. At the first possible opportunity she raced to see him. It was in Holland, where Osel was visiting a centre with Maria. He was by then 17 months old. Osel took no notice of her at all. Not a glimmer of recognition – not a hint of the close bond that had been forged between her and Lama Yeshe over the years. Hurt and disappointed, Suzanna deduced that it must be because she had not followed the Buddhist path diligently enough. 'Well, I guess I have been a bad student,' she said to a nearby monk. At that the monk turned to Osel who was crawling on the floor and said 'You remember Suzanna, don't you?' Osel stood up, put his baby arms in the air, swung them back and forth and tried to click his fingers, as though dancing. No one present, except possibly Osel himself, could understand why such a simple gesture should make Suzanna once again burst into tears. This was all the proof she needed. Lama Yeshe had kept his word. He had not forsaken her.

Max Redlich, the Australian monk who had been present with the cameras at Osel's formal testing in Dharamsala, was treated to his own informal ceremony later. Max had had a colourful past before becoming ordained. His parents emigrated from Austria to Australia, where they started a butcher's business which became immensely successful. Max joined the family firm which gave him the rare experience of wading (in wellington boots) knee-high in blood (terrific for later Buddhist meditations!). It also provided him with lots of money with which he bought his own plane, and the jet-set lifestyle to go with it. At one stage Zionist fervour interrupted this dazzling existence and he set off to Israel to fight in the Six-Day War. There he became deaf in one ear, from being too close to exploding shells, and learnt face to face what death was (also terrific for later Buddhist meditations). This kind of character was right up Lama Yeshe's street, and Max became his driver in Dharamsala for a time.

Max takes up the story: 'Lama Yeshe had a new jeep for going up the steep road to the Tushita Retreat Centre. For two years before he passed away I would take the jeep down to Pathankot station to meet him. The first thing Lama Yeshe would do when he arrived at Tushita would be to go round the jeep, inspecting it with me, giving me advice and suggestions about its maintenance. The year before he died the same procedure was followed. In particular Lama noted a scratch on one side he wanted fixed, he also wanted the back number plate, which was broken, replaced.

'One day, after Osel had gone through those traditional tests with Lama Zopa (which were quite something to witness), I was in the garden with a group of people at Tushita. Osel came out of the house, came straight for me, took me by the hand and led me over to the jeep which was parked in its usual place in the driveway. He began to walk me round it, slowly, looking at everything, pointing it all out in grunts. I couldn't believe it was happening. This was a baby in nappies! When we got to the back he saw the back number plate, which still hadn't been fixed, looked up at me and scowled! He kept on walking, leading me by the hand. We got to the front of the jeep which had a brand-new number plate, for some reason. Osel shook my hand, looked at me and beamed. I flipped. If what was happening was what I thought was happening, this child was showing me he had total recall of events which had happened in his past life. It was mind-blowing,' he said.

Everyone who saw Osel was having to think what exactly reincarnation was. Something was definitely going on – there was now too much evidence for it all to be dismissed as 'coincidence' – but Osel clearly wasn't an exact replica of Lama Yeshe. He had his own personality traits, not all of which were 'holy', and he didn't look like Lama Yeshe, being Spanish and under two years old.

Thankfully, the Gelugpa sect of Tibetan Buddhism, of which Lama Yeshe was a member, encouraged debate and questioning of all 'truths' presented, on the grounds that if one couldn't be personally convinced after thorough and genuine examination, that truth should be thrown out. To me this had always seemed fair enough.

Thubten Pende is an American monk studying for the geshe degree at the FPMT's Nalanda monastery in France. He is, by inclination and training, a scholar of piercing intellect. When Osel arrived at Nalanda with his mother he received a warm welcome. He seemed to feel at home immediately, happily falling in with the daily routine of life in a western Tibetan Buddhist monastery. One evening Pende, who was not personally convinced of Osel's identity as Lama Yeshe's reincarnation, decided to hold his own test. He got a pair of sun-glasses that had once belonged to Lama Yeshe and placed them on a table, along with four or five other pairs belonging to other people. He said nothing, but waited to see if Osel would do anything. Osel came into the room and after a while wandered over to the table. He looked at the sun-glasses and played with them for a bit. He then got hold of the pair belonging to Lama Yeshe, walked over to Pende and hit him over the head with them. The intellectual was literally having his proof drummed into him. All the monks who had been enjoying this silent performance applauded.

Californian nun, Thubten Angmo, had known Lama Yeshe since 1973 and had a particularly close relationship with him. Her background had not been dissimilar to Zina Rachevsky's, the Russian 'princess'. Thubten Angmo, or Heather Meston, to use her 'real' name, had also come from a rich Hollywood background. Her mother, a model and actress, and her father, a scriptwriter, had divorced when she was five, and Angmo had found the only source of stability in her grandmother, a woman who had lived in China, and taught her the philosophies of the East. Angmo therefore grew up with a natural inclination towards Buddhism and a belief in reincarnation.

Having met the lamas, her path was set. In 1982 she decided to do a three-year retreat. Lama Yeshe agreed and designed for her a small but comfortable house in the grounds of the Tushita Retreat

Centre, in Dharamsala, complete with roof garden, hot water, a modern kitchen and courtyard. 'You're a Californian girl and should be comfortable – if your mind is happy you can stay in retreat for a long time,' he argued. He also gave her the tantric deity Vajrayogini, as her special meditational practice. When he was at Dharamsala he would visit Angmo several times a week in her retreat to supervise her progress.

Angmo met Osel in Holland. She was delighted when she was asked to babysit one afternoon. That same day she had just bought three photographs of Tibetan deities and had put them on the bed. When Osel arrived he went over to the bed, picked up a photograph and thrust it very strongly, face down, on Angmo's heart. When she looked at it she saw that Osel had chosen the one of Vajrayogini. 'It was such a specific thing to do – so direct. Osel knew what he was doing. It certainly convinced me! This was Lama giving me my deity again,' she said.

To others, Osel appeared in dreams long before actual contact was made. Swedish nun Yeshe Chodron (Ingeborg Sandberg), now resident at Osel-Ling in Bubión, saw a fair-haired child with his dark-haired mother very clearly one night while she was sleeping. The father was in the background, less distinct. The child particularly caught her attention. He was three years old with golden blond hair and a slightly receding chin. In the dream he came to Inge and indicated that he wanted to be lifted up. She put the child on her hip, he looked her straight in the eye and said, 'I am your guru.' When she woke, Inge was haunted by the dream, which left a deep impression on her. It was not the confused type of dream she usually had – this one had a different quality. She was convinced that some day she would make contact with the child that had appeared to her. Then she realized that Serkong Rinpoche, one of her teachers, had just died, and became convinced that the child was him. Lama Yeshe was in fact still alive at this time.

Later she saw a picture of Maria, Paco and Osel and recognized the child immediately. That's him, she thought. That's Serkong Rinpoche! Inge persisted in believing that Osel was the reincarnation of Serkong Rinpoche until finally persuaded otherwise. Lama Zopa sent her to Osel-Ling, where she had plenty of opportunity to be with the child who had appeared to her so prematurely in her dream.

Above: The test. Fourteen-month-old Osel is asked by Lama Zopa Rinpoche to select the bell belonging to the late Lama Yeshe. The correct choice helped to confirm his true identity.

Below: Osel travelling in mufti during his first major overseas tour – to California, to visit the place where he had 'died' and been cremated in his previous life.

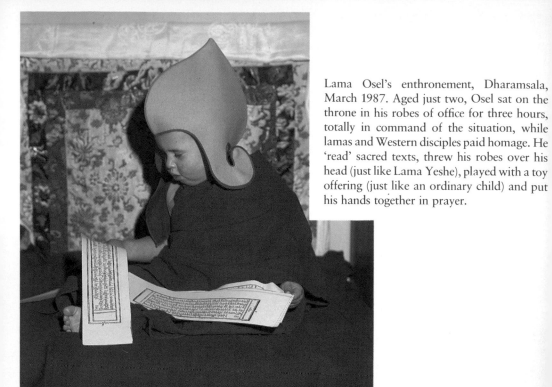

Lama Osel's enthronement, Dharamsala, March 1987. Aged just two, Osel sat on the throne in his robes of office for three hours, totally in command of the situation, while lamas and Western disciples paid homage. He 'read' sacred texts, threw his robes over his head (just like Lama Yeshe), played with a toy offering (just like an ordinary child) and put his hands together in prayer.

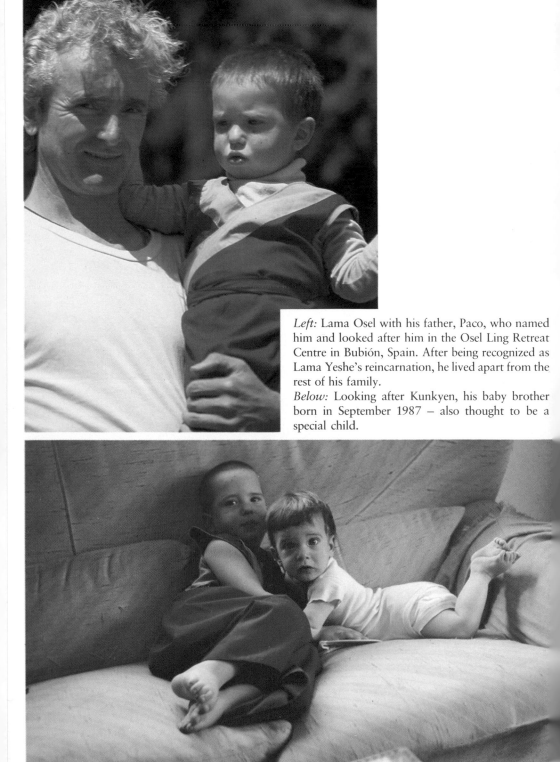

Left: Lama Osel with his father, Paco, who named him and looked after him in the Osel Ling Retreat Centre in Bubión, Spain. After being recognized as Lama Yeshe's reincarnation, he lived apart from the rest of his family.

Below: Looking after Kunkyen, his baby brother born in September 1987 – also thought to be a special child.

Sunday with the family in Bubión, Spain: Osel with his parents, Maria and Paco, and siblings Yeshe, Harmonia, Lobsang and Dolma.

Above: The last sad meeting. Vicki Mackenzie with Lama Yeshe on the path outside meditation tent in Kopan in 1983, just after he had given his last great teachings on love compassion. Three months later he was dead.

Below: Another meeting, another path. Three years later, in Bubión, Spain, Vicki Macke finds herself holding the hand of the new Lama Yeshe, Lama Tenzin Osel Rinpoche.

'I didn't need proof, of course – after what I'd experienced, but I did need to re-establish the feeling I used to have with Lama Yeshe,' she told me. 'One day Osel was being carried by one of the monks who said to him, "Give Inge your blessing." Osel reached out, stroked my cheek and got hold of my chin in one movement, just the way Lama Yeshe used to do. It was intimate and so affectionate. The same close wonderful feeling I used to get with Lama Yeshe. I knew after my dream that Osel was a special child, but that personal contact meant a lot to me. It was exactly what I needed,' she said.

'After that I noticed Osel would somehow mirror my mind. When I was in a good frame of mind I could feel the contact again; when I was negative I would lose it and Osel seemed just an ordinary baby. But that's how it was with Lama. When I was feeling negative I'd lose contact with him, too – it was as if he couldn't reach me.'

Zia Bassam, also a nun, had a very rich dream life which she claimed always proved remarkably accurate. This fascinating, small, dark Egyptian woman who'd been born in Calcutta and educated in India, the Middle East, Scotland and London, had spent four years travelling with Lama Yeshe as his cook and general housekeeper. The bond between them grew strong, with both of them enjoying the same things – cooking, flowers, the home environment, the 'feminine' side of life. Zia always discussed her dreams with him and frequently found him appearing in them, usually as a guide.

'When he was sick in America I had a very clear dream of him – there was a crowd of people and Lama Yeshe was in the sky above them all, looking happy, but definitely removed. I knew from this he was going to die,' explained Zia. 'But as he looked down he said "I am going to come back to help." Later in Dharamsala, while I was in retreat and Lama Zopa was looking everywhere for the reincarnation, he kept asking me if I had had any dreams. I kept saying I hadn't. Towards the end of the retreat I did have a dream in which I saw a child, aged six or maybe eight, running through the woods with the most ecstatic expression of joy on his face. I particularly noticed the eyes, which were dark and rather close together, and the nose which was unusually short. He was wearing maroon shorts and a pale yellow T-shirt, the colour of our robes. It was Osel's face, but an older Osel.

'When I saw Lama Zopa return to Dharamsala with a small child being carried on a monk's shoulders I knew instantly he'd found his guru. Lama Zopa had changed. When he'd left he was looking tired, old and haggard. Now he looked so young, happy and was laughing, laughing. As I bent over with my hands together in front of Osel I saw his feet. I recognized them instantly as the feet of Lama Yeshe, even though he was just a toddler. Then I looked up and saw his face. It was the face of the child I'd seen in my dream. Those eyes and that nose are so distinctive you couldn't mistake them. Later I sat down in front of him and he looked at me for a split second with the eyes that were 100 per cent not the eyes of a child. They were the eyes of a very high being. It was a very piercing look, that saw right into me. It was no different from the way Lama Yeshe would look at me sometimes.

'The more I see of him the more I *know* he is a continuation of Lama Yeshe — and I believe he will prove it more and more as he grows older,' she said.

The evidence that Osel had strong connections with the late Lama Yeshe was rapidly growing. At Kopan, in Nepal, Trisha Donelly, an English woman who had lived and worked with Lama Yeshe for years and who is now undergoing the preliminary practices in preparation for a three-year retreat, always 'felt' that the child living in the monastery above her small house was Lama Yeshe.

'There are so many little things he does that are strongly reminiscent of Lama Yeshe — the way he walks, and moves, his love of flowers. The way he goes to the monks' rooms to see if they are all right. His mannerisms,' she said. 'He's also given me some very concrete proof. Lama Yeshe had made a special study of a Tibetan practice called "The Six Yogas of Naropa", which involved among other things certain highly esoteric and secret "yogas" — physical exercises, not at all like the yoga done in India and the West. Just after he'd arrived at Kopan Osel stood on the mound above my house, caught my eye, then swiftly, but deliberately did one of these secret yogas. I couldn't quite believe what I had seen. It wasn't an exercise you could mistake, but how could this small child know it? I checked with everybody on the hill to see of they had been practising the Six Yogas of Naropa. Nobody had. As far as I knew he hadn't seen anyone do them. Later he did it again. The third time he did it, just a few weeks ago, he was sitting in the garden in his underpants. Now he could speak. "Me doing exercise," he said and promptly did another secret yoga. This time it was unmistakable. I fully believe he is Lama Yeshe,' she said.

Another Kopan inmate, John Cayton, also known simply as Karuna, had escorted Lama Yeshe to Delhi when he was so ill. He had stayed with Lama until he had flown to California, during which time he had said repeatedly to Karuna, the mystifying words: 'I am you and you are Lama.' Karuna thought maybe Lama was indicating that soon he was going to be reborn and become a young man, while Karuna was going to get old, sick and die. But he never found out their true meaning. Recently Osel returned to Kopan and one day, while Karuna was walking underneath his window, he stuck his head out and shouted, 'I am you and you are Lama.' Again those mystifying words. 'Maybe one day I will find out what exactly he means,' he said.

'I certainly see flashes of Lama Yeshe, but the medium's different. We in the West still have to examine how these reincarnated high lamas operate. Do they have full awareness from birth? Or does the fact that they have taken birth at all impose certain limitations? I believe as a baby you have to have a baby's capacity, and that in reincarnated lamas' case the realizations are latent, not manifest. They need to be regained. According to what the Tibetans say, however, the process shouldn't take long. They just have to be taught once and they know it. It's going to be interesting to see,' he concluded.

Others were much more cautious in their appraisal of Osel Hita Torres. As one man, a writer, put it, 'I believe in rebirth, but I still haven't seen it. The heart says "yes", but the cerebal cortex says, "yes but".' He summed up what quite a few of Lama Yeshe's students were feeling. The point for many was that no matter how many indications Osel gave that he had a direct connection with the deceased lama there was no way you could scientifically prove that he was. For the doubters there would always be ample scope to prove their case as well.

Harvey Horrocks, who came to Kopan in the very early days and now runs the central office of the FPMT organization in Kathmandu, said, 'We must ask, "How is it you would expect to recognize Lama Yeshe?" It's an extremely subtle thing. Even if you get the miracles, will it still do the trick? Even if a guy levitates, for example, there will still be those who aren't satisfied and will want to look for the strings. And do we want hordes of people trekking up to Kopan, waiting to hear Osel say "In my last life I was born in a little village outside Lhasa" and so on? I'm hoping that whatever Osel is going to do it will demonstrate that he is benefiting sentient beings.'

The Californian students, who had such a special relationship with Lama Yeshe, also had some interesting things to say on the matter. They had had the extraordinary experience of seeing Osel come to Vajrapani on the occasion of the consecration of the Stupa dedicated to his previous incarnation. Their reaction was an honest combination of scepticism and faith.

'I didn't see it, but I believe it,' said Age Delbanco, a Danish student of Buddhism, now living in California. 'My feeling is that a reincarnated lama is only his enlightened energy, not his personality. Osel is not Lama Yeshe come back, it's Lama Yeshe's energy in a new form. With Osel I don't experience the strong connection I had with Lama Yeshe, the same relationship, but I don't expect to. I could see that Osel was not an ordinary kid. He was definitely special. No other 20-month-old kid could receive the amount of attention Osel was getting and not take advantage of it. Osel was on top of it all, not oblivious to it, merely accepting it. I watched him – everything he did seemed to come from within. Yet he gave me no personal proof. Frankly I didn't need it. I got everything I needed from Lama Yeshe,' he said.

Beverly Gwynn, who had diligently nursed Lama Yeshe during his last weeks of life, told me, 'I can't say I felt he was Lama Yeshe, but when Osel arrived I did sense that Lama's energy was back here again. I also noticed that I felt around Osel how I felt around Lama. One morning I saw him go into the Gompa and walk over to where Lama Yeshe's body had been laid out in the coffin and start doing prostrations – which was fairly amazing. Later, during a puja when we started doing the mandala offering he came to sit by me and started piling sand up in my shoes, as though he were making his own mandala. Then he took my hand – and I did feel a close bond, but it was not the sign that I had been looking for. Maybe it will happen when he's older,' she said.

Tom Waggoner, who had been with Lama Yeshe when he

actually passed away, naturally scrutinized Osel very closely when he came to Vajrapani, although for him, like everyone else, this was such a new phenomenon he didn't know what to expect. He first saw Osel in the arms of Lama Zopa. 'I came towards him with my hands together and Lama Zopa says, "Give Tom a blessing." Osel blesses me on my head, then pulls my beard. As I turn to leave Osel calls me back, and pulls on my beard again. Lama Zopa, smiling, says, "He remembers you." I was somewhat in awe, thinking that I was now experiencing the other end of reincarnation. But my mind is also sceptical. Somewhere was the thought, "Is this really it?". I wanted to have total faith, to surrender completely, but it's a big job. To truly believe one dies and is reborn, as we are taught, would involve a big awakening in one's being. So I still had my doubts. Later, walking along a path with Lama Zopa, he remarked that Osel *did* recognize me.

'I replied, "Really – do you *truly* think he did?" And Lama Zopa looks at me with eyes like swords, wrathful: "Of course – how could you doubt!" he said, deeply shocked. But although my mind couldn't accept it totally it was still something to marvel about. This wasn't Lama Yeshe, it was Osel – here with Lama Zopa. We were all together again and I had witnessed the whole process,' said Tom.

It was Lennie Kronisch, however, who had arguably the richest experiences to report. Lennie, a qualified nurse and psychologist, had also been called in to lend her considerable skills in looking after Lama in those last weeks of his life, when he was so desperately ill. As she recounted, he stretched her to the very limits of her personal endurance. Osel was to do the same again. Lennie's account of his visit was all the more interesting because not only was she a mother of three, but during the course of her work she had attended literally thousands of births and was a child-care and development expert. Her view of Osel was tinged with her professional experience.

'From the beginning there was obviously something different about this child. My first impression was that he wasn't endearing! That surprised me, and made me feel a little guilty. I had expected that a child who was a rinpoche – a reincarnation of Lama Yeshe who was so radiant – would have an exceptionally beautiful face; angelic-looking. This child was not like that at all. His head was larger than other children of his age, in shape and size. It looked like a man's head on a toddler's body. There was a strange maturity about his face, too. He didn't look like a toddler of 20 months. In fact he didn't look like a child at all. He looked like a small man. Osel was young and old at the same time.

'He was very serious. He hardly smiled. There was something riveting about him in that way, but something unnerving too. There was nothing about him that would make me respond to him the way I normally would with a baby. I'm not a cutsie-putsie, itsy-kitsie person with children at all, but there was a quality about this child that was very unusual right from the start. And it wasn't charming, enticing, enchanting or beautiful. It was a *power*. A power without smiling. He was able to exert a lot of influence with a grunt. Not like an ordinary child who would point and make noises. *He* would point at something with certitude, knowledge and power. He was accustomed to commanding. I saw authority in that infant body.

'But, as I said, there was nothing infantile about him. I had met a lot of incredible children during my career and in the 10 years that I've been following a spiritual path, but I had never met a child like him,' she said.

As Lennie watched and discussed her confused feelings with a close friend who'd also come to see the new incarnation, Maria asked if she would mind babysitting one evening while they attended some lectures Lama Zopa was giving. Lennie happily agreed. Maria explained that Osel would be asleep when she arrived and that he never woke up. In the unheard-of event that he did wake, however, there would be a bottle of milk at the head of the bed. Lennie duly arrived at 7.30 p.m. at the little wooden cabin where the family was staying, and found Osel fast asleep in the sleeping loft upstairs, as Maria had said. She settled down to write some letters.

Then suddenly she heard crying. She climbed the vertical stairs to find Osel sitting up in bed screaming his head off – nose running, eyes running, in a terrible state. She handed him the bottle of milk and he flung it out of her hand across the room and *ordered* her off his bed! The nightmare began. Osel climbed out of bed and headed for the stairs. Lennie rushed after him – the stairs were steep, with no handrail and there was a burning wood stove directly underneath. Osel insisted on going down. Lennie, in despair, picked him up and somehow carried the screaming, kicking child down those treacherous stairs. Nothing she could do would soothe him. She pulled out every trick in her mothercare book. He would have none of it.

Finally she wrapped a blanket around him and went outside. Immediately he began to calm down. He stopped sobbing. She walked him up and down, singing to him. He began to cave in against her chest and allowed her to give him the bottle. Her back was in agony, so was her hip and neck – Osel was a very heavy child, and Lennie had been in a head-on collision in her car the week before – and so she put her foot up on a rail to rest. (If she started to sit down, Osel began crying again.) And as she stood in that awkward position, with the bottle in her hand feeding Osel, he reached up, grabbed her shirt and pulled her closer to him.

'It was exactly the same scene as I'd lived through with Lama Yeshe. Me stuck in the same agonizing position, feeding him, being stretched to the ends of my physical and emotional limits by the guru, and him pulling me to him by my shirt. It all came back as though it were yesterday. Then Osel reaches up with his other hand and starts twisting my hair in his fingers, in the same affectionate, intimate gesture that Lama Yeshe would do. This was something only Lama Yeshe knew! I couldn't believe it was happening. It was such incredible proof.'

Osel hadn't finished with Lennie yet. The woman who gave so much of herself was suddenly getting a lot back. The next day Lennie took Osel for a walk through the woods and her initial intuitive impression that here was a child of advanced intelligence was confirmed. 'I would point out things in nature, which is what I like to do with children, and I was astonished by the quickness of his mind and his perception. After a while he could identify different bird song! This was exceptional.

'We walked up to the ridge where Lama Yeshe had been cremated. He didn't take any notice of the burnt remains of the Stupa, but as we walked away to go down to lunch and see his parents – he pulled me and another woman back. He headed for an old, extremely shabby carpet, which was half-buried in the ground, which we used to sit on to say prayers for months after Lama Yeshe died. Osel made us all sit down on it, in a row, just like we used to. It was a strange thing to do. The carpet itself could have had no interest to a child — it wasn't pretty, had no toys on it — and there were his parents and lunch waiting for him down the hill. Once again he'd engineered a moment of profound significance, one that wasn't easy to explain away,' she said.

The stories of Osel's unusual behaviour continued as I followed his progress around the world, both literally and mentally. The living example of reincarnation that we had been presented with was doing his job admirably. For whether we saw Lama Yeshe in him or not, he was without doubt making us, and a fair proportion of the world's population, question our habitual belief that this material world, including our bodies and brains, is the sum total of our reality. Lama Yeshe had once said, 'Buddhism is not comfortable. It should *shake*!' Osel, even though he could not yet speak, was certainly doing that. And often when I looked at him, I could hear Lama's voice during that last teaching in Kopan saying, 'Am I this body, this appearance? Who am I?'.

13

THE ENTHRONEMENT

The next time I saw Osel was in the middle of March 1987 on the occasion of his enthronement. The enthronement had originally been planned to take place in Kopan and, after not too much deliberation, the thought of seeing Lama Yeshe's reincarnation once again installed in his headquarters was sufficiently enticing to overcome misgivings about the extravagance of flying so far for just one event.

I arrived in Kathmandu and for the first time headed not for the monastery on the hill but for the relative luxury of a small new hotel in among the winding alleyways of Thamel, the colourful bazaar area of Kathmandu. Having showered and changed, I eagerly telephoned the FPMT Central Office for final details of the enthronement. The embarrassed tones at the other end immediately indicated that something was badly wrong. After a lot of discussion it emerged that it wasn't definite that the enthronement was going to be held at Kopan. In fact it wasn't definite that the enthronement was going to happen at all. At the moment Osel was in Dharamsala with his family and Lama Zopa was sorting out what was best for everyone. I was rendered speechless by this bombshell. I'd come so far, spent so much money, and even had a commission from a German magazine to cover the event, just to be met with what appeared to be typical eastern inefficiency and vagueness.

For the next week I and many other people, including several journalists who'd flown in from across the world to witness the event, were kept in suspense. One minute it was announced that the enthronement was going to be held in Dharamsala, the next that Osel was coming to Kopan. The tension was excruciating. I became increasingly exasperated and upset, and when I eventually met Lama Zopa on the path outside the Gompa one afternoon in Kopan I complained. He laughed. 'It will all make for a richer experience,' he said cryptically. Unbeknown to me, the dilemma was not caused by some capricious whim on the part of Lama Zopa but by visa complications for Osel (which were later sorted out). After a few more days of shifting venue – during which time we were mollified by some wonderful teachings given by Lama Zopa – it was finally announced that the enthronement was definitely on, in Dharamsala.

Panic! We rushed to various travel agents and the Indian visa offices, our hearts in our mouths in case we didn't make it to Dharamsala in time. It was a long, complicated journey, across India, and north through the turbulent Punjab into the very topmost peak of the subcontinent. To make matters worse, it was Holi Week, one of the largest religious festivals in India, and it seemed that every seat on plane and train had been booked up weeks before. Every day we dashed over to the travel agents to see if there were cancellations and at the eleventh hour I miraculously got on a plane to Delhi. The cost of this trip, along with my anxiety, was rapidly mounting. There were two days before the ceremony was planned to begin.

After a few hours' sleep in the bustling, noisy capital, I rushed through the streets to Old Delhi station to try to get a seat on a train which would take me and my travelling companions to Pathankot, the nearest railway station to Dharamsala. Stepping over countless sleeping bodies who seemed to have taken up permanent residence in the station, I made my way to the reservation office which already had a sizeable crowd waiting outside for the doors to open. In Holi Week all the mighty millions of India were obviously on the move. When the doors were finally unbolted we surged forward as one. In the mêlée I was somehow pushed to one desk, where a patient railway clerk consulted a timetable which looked as complicated as a computer manual, and much to my astonishment offered us the last remaining six seats in a train leaving that night – just enough for me and my travelling companions. It was a sleeper – third class, non-air-conditioned.

Returning that night with my fellow-travellers to the unbelievable chaos of Old Delhi station, I clambered aboard the filthiest train I'd ever seen and discovered to my horror that our 'sleeping' compartment consisted of *wooden* seats which converted into beds. It also had no door, and in fact no division from the countless other bodies all crammed into the corridor as if they were cattle. The attachment to the inner-spring mattress once again rose in my mind. I was now finally beginning to believe the fundamental Buddhist tenet that attachment, any attachment, only causes suffering. Through the night we trundled in enforced intimacy with Indian humanity (who in the way of their race accepted all life's conditions with uncomplaining passivity), the journey broken by frequent stops and a constant stream of food vendors offering their wares in vessels that hadn't seen washing-up liquid for the best part of a year.

The lavatory was another experience – a fetid enclosure where you balanced your feet on either side of a gaping hole, watching the railway tracks swinging perilously beneath. At least I didn't have Delhi belly. Instead I'd come down with flu. I was hot and my nose was running like a Delhi railway porter. Memories of those romantic films and travel documentaries extolling the mysteries of going by train through the Indian countryside flashed before my eyes. Were we in the same country?

At 10 a.m. the next morning I stepped out at Pathankot station, red nose co-ordinating nicely with my eyes. After a 'safe' breakfast of boiled eggs in the restaurant at this friendly station, with bougainvillea climbing the pillars and orange-sellers on the platforms, we piled into two taxis and negotiated the fare for the four-hour drive up the mountain to Dharamsala. Inevitably one car broke down and the other ran out of oil, as is the way with Indian taxis, but since we were travelling in tandem we came to each other's rescue, and by now I was resigned to the traumas of travel on the subcontinent. At last we drove past the little English church where Lord Elgin is buried, and entered a world of little Tibet. Here the thousands of Tibetans who followed their leader into exile, choosing to become refugees rather than suffer under Chinese rule, have over the past 25 years resurrected their own culture with considerable success.

With the Dalai Lama's residence as its spiritual centrepiece (a modest bungalow contrasting starkly with the mighty Potala Palace where he once lived) Dharamsala now boasts a large, golden-roofed temple, housing a giant statue of Chenrezig, the Buddha of Compassion (with His thousand arms reaching out to help all sentient beings), of whom His Holiness is said to be an emanation. There are also several thriving monasteries, where monks of the four schools of Tibetan Buddhism continue to keep alive their rich spiritual heritage of learning, debate and meditation, as well as the Tibetan Library of Works and Archives, housing some of the priceless ancient texts smuggled out of Tibet and thus rescued from the atrocities of the Chinese invasion, and the Medical Institute, now headed by Dr Tenzin Choedak. (He is the Dalai Lama's personal physician and was recently released after 20 years' imprisonment and torture by the Chinese for unspecified 'crimes'.) He is now busily engaged in preserving the ancient science of Tibetan medicine. Dharamsala also has a school of Arts and Drama and a thriving crafts industry where carpets and artefacts are made and sold.

It was good to be here again. The air was pure and the view of the plains below and the range upon range of snow-capped Himalayas behind was breathtaking. But the best thing of all was that we had arrived in time. The enthronement was to take place at the Tushita Retreat Centre the next afternoon.

At the appointed hour we all solemnly filed into the main meditation room of the Tushita Centre, wondering what was in store. There were about 60 of us in all, a motley crew, comprising monks, nuns, former students of Lama Yeshe and a large press corps, representing some of the most influential newspapers, magazines and press agencies in the world. All had trekked up the steep mountain road to witness and record an event which was by anyone's standards big news – the investiture of the world's smallest and most unusual lama ever. Osel Hita Torres, aged two years and one month, was about to make his official world début.

The Gompa had been specially festooned for the occasion. Richly coloured tankas, depicting aspects of the Buddha, covered every inch of the walls. The throne, three feet high, was draped with bright brocades. On the floor, on either side of the central aisle, sat two rows of Tibetan lamas in full ceremonial regalia. Behind them sat the western monks and nuns, and in whatever space was left sat the rest of us.

Long horns boomed, cymbals clashed, drums and damarus sounded, conch shells trumpeted in the eerie and evocative ritual of dispelling evil forces and summoning the Buddhas and protectors of the ten directions. And as the lamas began their massed chorus of deep-throated mantra – that sound which reaches far beyond ordinary emotion and thus touches the very inner core of your being – Osel arrived, carried in his father's arms.

I, for one, wasn't prepared for what I saw. Osel was dressed in full coronation regalia. He wore the ceremonial lama's robes and on his head was the high, crested, yellow pandit hat, the badge of office. Perhaps it was because he looked so little under that grand yellow hat or maybe it was the silence that fell on all of us as he entered, but the moment was undeniably moving. I noticed as he went past that he was sucking a sweet, and under his arm he carried a fluffy clockwork owl – a reminder that he was after all hardly more than a baby. He nodded to the posse of photographers gathered in one corner, like one who is used to dealing with the press, and after a second of protest allowed Paco to seat him on the throne.

There he perched, a tiny figure, the focus of all the attention, with his big hat endearingly slipping over his eyes from time to time and his owl rocking incongruously to and fro beside him. At his feet, to his right, sat his closest disciple, Lama Zopa, his face solemn with the import of the occasion. Beside the throne sat his parents, looking both proud and anxious. Staging a public ceremony with a two-year-old as its centrepiece was for them not only nerve-racking but fraught with potential disasters.

They had no cause for worry. For the next three hours Osel sat on his throne watching the proceedings with a stillness, composure and majesty that went far beyond his years. Two or three times he clambered down from his throne, once to sit on Paco's knee for a minute, then to play with a small Italian boy he'd spotted in the congregation, but he didn't object when Paco or his monk attendant gently replaced him on his seat. More surprisingly, he handled the photographers, who were flashing their cameras throughout the entire three hours, with consummate ease. Occasionally when he thought they were getting greedy he'd hold out a commanding hand and say 'No', but for the most part he was astonishingly accommodating, at times even posing for them. They, for their part, were beyond themselves with glee. Children and animals won any reader, and this child was a natural. They couldn't go wrong.

For those who understood the subtler points of Buddhism the

event took on deeper significance when they realized that here was Lama Yeshe's reincarnation, sitting on his former throne, in his former house, sleeping in his former bed, walking round the garden he had planted and using the same religious implements. To the believers, Osel was not just a novelty, a Spanish child being hailed as a lama, but the living proof of the continuity of individual consciousness. Here before us once again was the mind-stream of Lama Yeshe, albeit in another form, returned to this earth through his great compassion to help us all on our way to the truth. To compound the miracle, he had been recognized. How many saints, I wondered, had come amongst us quietly, their works and worth unsung until, perhaps, the moment they died? And that was fine, but somehow it did not give people the opportunity to take full advantage of their hallowed presence – to learn and perceive as much as they could.

Yet how fraught with danger was the position that Osel was now in. In publicly proclaiming his identity the Dalai Lama and Lama Zopa had exposed him to possible ridicule, controversy and even hostility from anyone who chose to attack him. How vulnerable he was. And how brave of His Holiness and Lama Zopa to stick their necks out in such a fashion – they must have been absolutely sure of what they were doing.

Right now Osel was handling himself and the situation as though he had indeed been born to it. He sat, dignified, on his throne while the ritual was carried on before him. He was offered Tibetan tea, which he drank with relish, and a host of other symbolic gifts: a gold-plated Dharmachakra (wheel) symbolizing the request for the guru always to give teachings; the Kangyur and Tengyur (the 108 volumes of the teachings of the Buddha and their commentaries); statues of Amitayus and Namgyalma (the Buddhas of Long Life); the robes and pandit hat of a Tibetan lama and five Dakini dresses symbolizing the wisdom goddesses of the five elements and their robes which Tibetan lamas don to perform their stylized, ritual dance.

The high point of the ceremony was when the lamas, led by Lama Zopa Rinpoche, lined up before him, did prostrations to him in homage and then humbly offered the child their gifts. Without prompting, Osel took each gift, placed the holy object on the crown of his head, in the lamas' way of showing reverence, and then handed it to his attendant. That done, he placed a chubby hand on the bowed head before him in blessing. He did it again and again – through the entire ranks of the Tibetan hierarchy and then the rows of westerners. I noticed he deviated once from this action when instead of reaching out his hand he bent forward and touched crowns with a young, handsome Tibetan lama, a mark of great respect. I later found out that this was Yang Tse Rinpoche, a recognized reincarnation of a former teacher of Lama Yeshe in Sera monastery in Tibet.

It was a staggering performance. By now Osel was clearly getting tired (although one westerner's gift of an ambulance with flashing red light obviously lifted his energy for a while) but he sat through it until the end. When the last hymns of praise had been sung, and the dedication that all the goodness accumulated be given to all sentient beings, Paco lifted him off the throne and took him out. Lama Zopa had been right. In spite or because of the hardships and effort invested in getting there, the enthronement was a rich experience indeed.

After that mammoth performance, Osel was spent. His parents reported that he wouldn't go into the Gompa where the enthronement had taken place, let alone sit on the throne. I couldn't say I blamed him. But a few days later, hoping for exclusive photographs for the German magazine assignment, I dared ask if Osel would be prepared to get back into his full ceremonial regalia and pose for the photographer, Robin Bath (an ex-student of Lama Yeshe) who had flown out from England to cover the event. Much to our surprise and delight, he agreed and we were privileged enough to receive our own private photo session.

If Osel had shone during the official enthronement, he excelled himself for Robin's camera. Back on the throne he went through the gamut of Lama Yeshe's facial expressions, all for Robin's camera. He looked serene, holy, wise, mischievous, profound, compassionate and funny in turn. With extreme graciousness he took a piece of fruit from the offering bowl on the side of the throne and handed it to each person in the room – a gesture of caring and concern that was archetypally Lama Yeshe – but to stop the proceedings getting too pompous he then hurled an orange at Robin, and burst into giggles. At another point he threw his robes over his head, just like Lama used to do, and sat there – the ultimate clown. Then he got hold of a loose-paged Tibetan text, placed it in front of him on the throne and proceeded to 'read' it with the sing-song voice of a Tibetan lama, turning the pages over and placing them in a neat pile before him. It was impressive! After that he put his hands in the meditation posture, closed his eyes and began to say mantras. It was Lama Yeshe, synthesized and in miniature.

The pictures revealed what a special moment it was, but unfortunately the German magazine didn't use them or the story. They were too pressurized by Osel's story bursting into print across Europe to wait for our exclusive material. Although the press coverage overall was favourable and unbiased, there was the inevitable journalist who lapsed into sensationalism, or did not get the facts right, and one who was downright scurrilous. An Indian newspaper said that 'sources' in Dharamsala had revealed that Osel had not been recognized by the Dalai Lama and that the whole story was in part a ruse to get funds for Kopan. This was later repudiated by Lama Zopa and the Dalai Lama himself, and the so-called 'sources' could not be identified. It was the only brickbat hurled at Osel. I wondered how many more he would have to face throughout his life.

After the big event was over, and Osel was left to play in the garden and throw stones in the pond like a normal child, I decided I might as well take advantage of the other opportunities that landing in Dharamsala had brought. By complete coincidence, the day after the enthronement the Dalai Lama began teaching an extensive Lam Rim text to a large audience to Tibetan pilgrims who had spent weeks *walking* over the Himalayas to be in the presence of the living Buddha, their spiritual and temporal leader. How feeble my exertions in catching a plane and train seemed in comparison. Sitting on the grass outside the main temple they were a splendid sight. The women wore their long traditional dresses wrapped over at the back, their brightly striped aprons, their long black hair plaited with coloured threads and ribbons and their best jewellery – large pieces of amber and turquoise dangling at their ears or woven into their hair. The men, with their high boots, brocade fur-trimmed hats, and coats worn nonchalantly over one shoulder, were impressive too. They were a good-looking race, proud and strong, but with a gentleness, humour and humility that come from deeply ingrained spirituality.

They listened to the Dalai Lama's teachings through a loud-speaker system. The hierarchy of Tibetan lamas, geshes and rin-poches sat inside the temple, those higher in spiritual status sitting closer to His Holiness. And a group of us westerners sat in haphaz-ard rows in a space allotted to us on the verandah just outside, gleaning the Dalai Lama's profound wisdom through simultaneous translation transmitted on FM radio. Here was the meeting of East and West – ancient wisdom and modern science. A good marriage. One that both the Dalai Lama and Lama Yeshe constantly advo-cated as being necessary for modern man.

In spite of the seriousness of the occasion it certainly wasn't solemn. During the breaks the entire congregation of hundreds were all provided with tea, brought by convoys of young monks wielding large silver kettles filled with either the salted butter tea for the Tibetans, or sweetened ordinary tea for us westerners. The breaks became like picnics, with people sharing food and getting to know their neighbours. And the Tibetans themselves, although devoted to their religion and leader, were not above throwing orange peel and pips at each other whenever the philosophy became too dry or difficult.

The Dalai Lama didn't mind a bit. He was utterly informal and relaxed himself – making frequent jokes (often at the expense of the monks), laughing, even yawning quite openly. He was completely himself – natural, unpretentious and warm beyond measure. No wonder his people loved him. Here was a leader who was not only supremely wise, but who reached out like a father to his people. In this guise, at least, he was infinitely human.

There were other people to see in Dharamsala as well. I'd been given a chance to see my first ever Tibetan child tulku – the young Trijang Rinpoche who had had such a galvanizing effect on Osel, when he first came to Dharamsala the year before. With Robin and his cameras to record the event, I made my way down the mountainside, past the large Tibetan Library and the rapidly ex-panding Medical Centre to a modest bungalow standing in a small garden, the home of the previous Trijang Rinpoche, tutor to the Dalai Lama.

Once again there was no formality. I hadn't made an appoint-ment but explained to a man at the gate who I was and what I wanted. He politely told me to wait for a few minutes. After a short time Robin and I were ushered into a room where a small Tibetan child sat on a low throne. His face was not only beautiful but charged with that strange authority and maturity I had seen in Osel. He accepted the white scarf I gave him, putting it back over my head, as is the custom, and then gave me a blessing cord from a large pile beside him. He did the same for Robin. It was all obviously routine, something he'd been doing for some time. Yet he was only four years old. He seemed much, much older. Then as he turned to a toy helicopter on the bench beside him, examining it with the detached scrutiny of a scientific mind, he relaxed, grinned and became visibly impish. It was like Osel – we'd seen the spiritual being, now we were being shown the child. He flicked a rubber band at Robin (who was by now getting a complex about rinpoches hurling missiles at him) and then at his attendant. He laughed in delight at the response he was getting.

The attendant decided he needed more space, so he lifted Trijang Rinpoche on his shoulders and carried him outside, the young boy hitting him playfully over the head as he went. I wasn't quite sure what to make of him. To my eyes he didn't have the sweetness that Osel had about him, but he was indisputably precocious and had a presence that was almost imperious. On one memorable occasion he stood in the garden, legs apart, hands on hips, striking a very regal pose. If he'd pointed a finger and said 'Obey!' I would not have been surprised. Trijang Rinpoche was only too aware of his position. When a young Tibetan couple arrived with their baby to pay homage, he stood silent, waiting for them to finish their prostrations, and then extended his hand in blessing. It was all so natural to him.

The story was told by his attendant Mr Panden. Trijang Rinpoche was the son of a carpet weaver, one of five children. His mother began to notice something strange about her third son when he continuously moved his right thumb very fast against his index finger – the movement a lama makes when counting his rosary beads. The child also had an enormous thirst for milk. When he was reprimanded for this on the grounds that it was an extravagance the family couldn't afford the young child replied nonchalantly that they were not to worry for he had a herd of eight cows in Dharamsala. They were mystified by this information

– and only discovered what he meant when he was recognized as the reincarnation of the late Trijang Rinpoche, who had indeed owned a herd of cows, eight to be exact.

The child won his position from no fewer than 500 candidates! (Most of their names were put forward by mothers who all thought their children showed special signs, and who coveted the prestigious position the title brought with it.) This staggering list was finally reduced to eight names and presented to the Dalai Lama, who after doing observations and prayers, reduced the names further to three. Deeper meditations and spiritual practices revealed the present child as the rightful reincarnation of Trijang Rinpoche. He then went through the strict series of tests of choosing his former objects, as Osel had done, and was instated as one of the highest authorities in the Tibetan hierarchy.

Returning to the former Trijang Rinpoche's house with his parents, the boy walked from room to room, saying, 'This is mine' about various things. He also took down a group photograph of several lamas and, pointing to Trijang Rinpoche, said clearly for all to hear: 'This is me.' Like Osel he has continued to make constant references to events and details of his former life.

'No one has any doubts,' said Mr Panden. He already attends the monastery for lessons and can recite several texts. He doesn't need to be taught the scriptures – just hearing them once, he can recite them back immediately. This is because he remembers. Other children in his class need to be told them many, many times. He has also mastered the English alphabet and numbers – and can now read a few simple English words,' he told us.

This was exciting news. With a European reincarnate lama poised to enter the Tibetan system, and a Tibetan reincarnate lama already learning the ways of the West, the cross-cultural interchange, which Lama Yeshe and the other high lamas had envisaged, might have begun. What riches they could bestow on each other's races.

Mr Panden, however, was wary about making predictions. 'We don't know yet whether he will teach again, as his predecessor did. There are expectations for him to do so. And the people of Tibet hope he will return there and grace his country with his presence. But who knows? We will have to wait and see what the future will bring,' he said cautiously.

His wariness was understandable. For all the diligence and thoroughness taken in searching out a reincarnation, there is always the possibility of a wrong, or unfortunate choice. The sixth Dalai Lama, for example, who assumed control of Tibet around 1700, showed little interest in either his political or religious duties, preferring to spend his time writing poems and fraternizing with the ladies. Nevertheless he remains a strong favourite among Tibetans who still sing his songs and loyally claim that 'eccentric' behaviour does not necessarily deny inherent spirituality.

More recently, both inside and outside Tibet, it is not unknown for reincarnate lamas to demonstrate a similar predilection for 'the good life' over the austerities of ascetic existence. Although this is tolerated and even permitted within some sects of Tibetan Buddhism, (the flesh not being as closely associated with the Devil as it is in Christianity) such behaviour would undoubtedly leave a disastrous impression on newly found Rinpoches coming to the West.

In the main, however, the system for identifying reincarnations is remarkably good. The principal title-holders within the Tibetan spiritual hierarchy more than live up to expectations. Indeed the qualities that they embody are so fine that it would be hard to imagine they were not born with them. And the training and demands on these rinpoches are so severe that if they did not possess special qualities they would more than likely collapse under the strain.

14

LAMA ZOPA SPEAKS

The meetings with the two young rinpoches, western and eastern, had increased rather than quenched my seemingly insatiable curiosity about the workings of rebirth. What a strange phenomenon it was! Although, admittedly, the 'feel' for it was gradually turning into something like a conviction, there were still many things I wanted to know. Armed with a list of questions, I made an appointment to see the one person who I knew would be able to furnish me with at least some of the answers – Lama Zopa Rinpoche, trained in the knowledge of the subject, a recognized reincarnation himself. He should know, if anyone.

Something very curious had been happening to Lama Zopa in the years since his greatest·friend and teacher had passed away. He was changing, rapidly and radically. The man whom I'd always regarded as the archetypal meditator – refined, ascetic, thin and ethereal – had metamorphosed into a round, strong, sturdy figure with chubby cheeks and a large, expansive chest. The transformation had begun, I was told, shortly after Lama Yeshe had died, when Lama Zopa emerged from a retreat in Dharamsala. But it wasn't only his body that was changing; his personality was, too. The once outwardly reserved, rather straight-faced, earnest young man was becoming almost extrovert – jolly, jovial and given to making jokes (even in teachings!). The contrast with his former behaviour was so sharp it made him appear almost frivolous.

It was as though Lama Zopa had somehow absorbed Lama Yeshe into himself. I couldn't with my rational mind understand what was going on, but on another level it made perfect sense that Lama Zopa should take on some of Lama Yeshe's qualities. He was now Commander-in-Chief of the vast organization Lama Yeshe had founded. He needed to be expansive and strong to take on the huge responsibility that it entailed. He needed to become outgoing and develop a thicker skin. On a less mundane level, I had always seen the Lamas as being two sides of the same coin – the perfect duo. How reasonable that if one should die the other would, of necessity, manifest the totality of that rich partnership. Lama Zopa I knew had the power to do it.

Now this supremely humble but great man was sitting on a cushion on the floor in a garden room at Tushita, beckoning me to sit beside him. After offering me tea and enquiring politely about my health we got on to the real purpose of my visit. The questions poured out. How convinced was he that the Spanish child Osel was the reincarnation of his beloved guru Lama Yeshe? How could he be sure? Lama Zopa smiled: 'After my many observations when I saw the baby crawling on the carpet at Osel-Ling, when he was just seven months old, I felt overwhelmingly that he was Lama. I had no doubts. I saw Lama there, in baby form.' He paused for a moment, wanting to make a further point. 'From that moment until now I feel how incredibly, how *unbearably* kind it was of Lama that he should take another form to guide us. It's difficult to express how kind that action is, how unbelievably brave,' he said, swallowing back an emotion that had obviously overtaken him. And I thought how true it was – to voluntarily take on a body with all the ills that attend it and to re-enter this world with all its anger, greed, hostility and violence was indeed a noble act.

I recalled the story an Italian monk had told me. In his last months in the East, before he came to Kopan that last time in 1983, Lama Yeshe had been in retreat in Dharamsala, and the Italian monk had taken the room next to his. Every night for 30 nights the monk had listened to Lama Yeshe crying – saying his prayers, doing his religious practices and crying. The monk soon realized he was weeping because he knew he was going to leave us – poignantly the tears were not for himself but for us, the deluded, suffering beings he was leaving behind. Such was his compassion. The courage to come back could only be born of love – a love that most of us couldn't begin to know the meaning of.

But now Lama Zopa was telling me of all the other incidents which reassured him that he had made the right choice. 'I see so many things that remind me of Lama. One of Lama Yeshe's main characteristics was that he could make the public so happy.

Whenever he was with a crowd of people he could lift them up. Osel is like that too. Other children his age get very shy usually in front of large numbers of people, but Osel is very brave – he goes out before them and makes them all laugh. He can't talk yet but still he makes everyone happy. Just like Lama. The important point is he does it on purpose. It's not common for a baby to make up his mind to make people laugh. With Osel it's deliberate.'

It was a fine point, but true. Osel could take the microphone and stand in front of a crowd of 100 people and make them laugh. Later he was to sit on thrones and deliberately clown.

'And then small things. Lama Yeshe always liked gardening, and at Tushita Lama Osel is always playing with the gardening tools and looking at the flowers. Lama walked with a stick – Lama Osel walks with a stick. Lama Yeshe rubbed his head – Lama Osel rubs his head the same way. And Lama Yeshe was always so caring about everyone, from me right down to the puppies. He looked after all of us. I see Osel doing the same things. He goes round checking to see if we are happy – he goes into the kitchen and lifts the lids of the pots, checking the food in exactly the same way as Lama Yeshe did.

'When we go travelling he recognizes many of the places where Lama Yeshe stayed. When we returned to the house in Santa Cruz with Mummy Max, Lama Osel went into the main room and then turned immediately, went down two steps in a corner of the room and went straight to the room where Lama Yeshe had stayed when he was sick. Maria, his mother, didn't even know those steps and that room were there. It wasn't obvious. He rolled on Lama Yeshe's bed and opened all the drawers – looking.

'Even though he's only two years old he's already showing he has a great deal of knowledge about spiritual practice. This comes from his past life,' Lama Zopa continued. 'These actions arise purely from his own initiative. To me he looks like a young boy acting like an old monk. He knows the custom of returning the katag (white scarf) to the giver, putting it over the person's head and placing it around the neck. And from the moment he arrived in Dharamsala he wanted to bless people. This was completely spontaneous. The first time I saw him do this was when he was in a car with me. The car was stopped and some people, Tibetans, came for a blessing. I put Lama Osel on my knee, rolled down the window and was about to put Lama Osel's hand on the people's heads, when he did it himself. These things bring tears to my eyes. In my view Osel's behaviour is rare, even among other incarnate lamas of his age,' he said.

Had the small child revealed any of the closeness Lama Yeshe had had with his nearest disciple? Lama Zopa looked quite bashful for a moment and replied modestly, 'When I was in Spain, after Lama Osel had been recognized, he would come to where I was sitting and climb up on to my lap quite often. Actually, I feel he has always been close to me, but after the examinations in Dharamsala he seemed even closer.' Lama Zopa was a master of understatement. I knew from several witnesses that Osel was absolutely devoted to Lama Zopa and vice versa.

The 40-year-old lama treated his newly found guru with a tenderness and protectiveness that was truly wonderful to see. He'd take him up in his arms, holding him as though he were the most precious thing on earth. In spite of this exquisite intimacy there was never one moment when Lama Zopa forgot who the child really was. He treated the toddler in nappies with the same deference and reverence that he had shown to Lama Yeshe. And just as he'd talked of Lama Yeshe 'manifesting sickness', when he was dying, he now referred to Osel being in the 'aspect of crawling', or the 'aspect of a baby'. He was forever the perfect 'heart disciple', bound to Lama Yeshe by ties of love and devotion that were beyond ordinary comprehension.

Now that he had been discovered, what did Lama Zopa plan to do with him? After all here was no regular Tibetan rinpoche. Would he fit into the typical monastic structure designed to furnish incarnate lamas with the best spiritual education possible? Was that his future anyway? If Lama Yeshe had wanted to be traditional would he not have been born into a Tibetan family? Osel was an original, a one-off. Lama Zopa showed that he was well aware of this. The plans he'd made for the child's future were wide-ranging.

'I want him to have an English-speaking attendant, as well as a Spanish one (so that he retains his knowledge of his mother tongue). Then gradually I want to introduce him to Tibetan so that he can get a thorough grounding in Buddhist philosophy. These teachings I think might take place at Kopan – where he will be close to his family. Apart from that I would like him to learn about the other major religions of the world. Later he must have a strong education in western science – mathematics, physics, chemistry – and for that he will go to the West. This way Osel will acquire a very wide view and will be able to benefit extensively so many sentient beings according to their needs,' he explained. The plan was staggering in its breadth and implications. Osel, it appeared, was destined to become a new-style Renaissance man – a spiritual superman. I hoped I would be around to see it.

But Lama Zopa was confident. 'As he grows up and begins to speak he will show us even more that will amaze us. And this of its own accord will lead to great devotion and belief among those who see and hear him. When he begins to teach, his words will be incredibly powerful. If he is healthy and lives long, he will bring much happiness to the world,' said Lama Zopa, his view necessarily tempered by the basic Buddhist tenet that we must never take how long we will live for granted.

But, I wanted to know, were Lama Yeshe and Lama Osel exactly one and the same person? Surely there were some differences that could be attributed to genetic material, different parents, and an already radically different lifestyle to the one Lama Yeshe had experienced. Lama Zopa closed his eyes and thought. Eventually he looked at me kindly and gave me his explanation: 'The beautiful rose plant that we see today is but a continuation of yesterday's plant. Similarly, Lama Osel's holy mind is a continuation of Lama Yeshe's holy mind.' He became more profound, delving deeper into the Buddhist explanation. 'You see, the consciousness associated with that particular body which was named by the Abbot in Tibet, Lama Yeshe – that same mental continuum associated with a western body born in Spain now bears the merely imputed label, Osel. It is the same continuity. For the West to understand reincarnation it is necessary to begin to understand mind. But the insubstantial, non-physical is difficult to understand,' he stated matter-of-factly.

We were back with that old question 'Who am I?' Are we our 'label', that name given to a group of physical and mental attributes, that according to the Buddhists is never permanent anyway, but constantly in a state of flux? Are we more, or less? The answers I knew could only come from meditation – using the mind to explore the mind. To set out on that journey into inner space must surely be the greatest adventure left to man. If I understood him correctly today's rose plant, although it bore the same essence as yesterday's rose, would have its own characteristics. Osel both was, and was not, Lama Yeshe. The source was the same but the manifestation was different.

Then I posed my old favourite – the question of conditioning. Surely bringing him into an environment where he was surrounded by all the paraphernalia of Tibetan Buddhism, and where people were prostrating before him, was wrongly forcing him to become a lama. Wouldn't it be far more convincing to leave him in his own environment and let his spiritual qualities emerge spontaneously? Lama Zopa, used to the cut and thrust of debate, enjoyed my question. He became animated in his effort to reply to my challenge.

'On the contrary these conditions only make what is already there more obvious. Bringing him to India and Nepal to be near Tibetan lamas will help prove who he is,' he said. 'I think Lama Osel will show his spiritual worth *more* in this environment. You see true rinpoches only have to be taught for a very short time before their former memory is woken, and then they are able to give teachings themselves. I have seen myself that when that happens incredible things come out of their mouths. They can explain points and answer questions which even the high geshes do not know. Very esoteric knowledge emerges. So being with high geshes and lamas can provide greater evidence for who they really are.

'But even if Lama Osel were left in the West, living a normal family life, he would still show who he was by his unusual spiritual actions. Bringing him to this environment only helps bring out those qualities quicker,' he said.

Later it came to me how sensible the system of recognizing reincarnated beings is. Most of us with a spiritual leaning (or any leaning for that matter) do not find a means of fulfilling it until we are quite old. But these high lamas don't waste time. They get on with the job they are good at from the age of four or five, thus being saved a lot of frustration and heartache at being caught up in lifestyles and occupations for which they were never intended. Their lives are utilized for the greater benefit of all, right from the start.

Back to Osel. Does he automatically recognize people he knew as Lama Yeshe? 'If there was a relationship, a connection in the past, then that will happen again, in part if not completely,' said

Lama Zopa. 'The stronger the relationship in the past, the more likely the connection in the future. I've already seen Lama Osel make a special effort with some students to whom he was very close in his past life – he gives them things, or singles them out in some way.'

One last question. Does Osel know he's Lama Yeshe? 'I think he might tell us later,' said Lama Zopa, smiling enigmatically.

My attempts to probe his own memories of his former life drew a blank. Did he have any recollections about his time in the cave meditating as the Lawudo Lama? 'Just darkness,' he replied curtly. Then he added, 'The consciousness is much clearer when you are younger.' It was all I could get from him. The visor of inscrutability had come down over his face, forbidding further investigation. Secretly I was pleased. This was the way of the truly skilful spiritual teacher – not dazzling his student with revelations of his own spiritual prowess – merely showing the path.

15

THE DALAI LAMA

On my voyage of discovery around reincarnation I had the extreme
good fortune on two occasions to be granted an audience with its
greatest living exponent, Tenzin Gyatso, the 14th Dalai Lama of
Tibet. By our calendar this intriguing but infinitely humble man,
who prefers to wear the ordinary maroon and gold robes of a
monk, is 53 years old. If you add together all his recognized
reincarnations, however, his age amounts to a staggering 598 years.
The mystery is further compounded when you appreciate that these
are no ordinary reincarnations, for the Dalai Lama is venerated by
some 14 million people around the world as a living Buddha – an
emanation of Chenrezig, the Buddha of Compassion, who made a
vow to protect all living beings. To the six million Tibetans, he is
born to be absolute spiritual and temporal leader of their country
and they worship him with a zeal that 30 years of Chinese communist anti-religious indoctrination has not diminished, but has, if
anything, fired.

On meeting him it is easy to see why. This slightly stooped man,
with a perpetual twinkle of mirth and good humour in his eye,
emanates a humanity which resonates with everyone he meets. He
is one of those rare souls whom it is virtually impossible to dislike.
And, in spite of his awesome position he is unnervingly informal,
dismissing with a wave of the hand any reverent approaches you
might make towards him.

Both times I have been to see him, once in the Dean of West-
minster's sitting-room in London, for an interview for the *Sunday
Times*, and once in his own modest bungalow in Dharamsala, he
has come towards me with his hand outstretched in greeting,
insisting I keep my shoes on, and has sat me down in a chair next
to his without the barrier of a desk that high officials usually like
to erect between themselves and the public, as though we were two

friends meeting for a chat. In London he even made me sit in the comfortable armchair while he perched on the harder high-backed chair – much to my initial embarrassment. I have interviewed many politicians and men and women of power, but I can say without any reservation that His Holiness the Dalai Lama is the most impressive person I have ever met. There is, absurdly, a cosiness about this living Buddha, as though you were encountering a wonderful friend with whom you felt entirely safe and relaxed, and to whom you could say anything.

And yet, paradoxically, his power is unmistakable. For all his humility you never forget for one second that you are truly in the presence of a Presence. You feel, underneath the easy charm, the ready giggle and the unpretentious manner, a flow of energy so potent that it is profoundly effective.

Suddenly that strange statue of Chenrezig with the many heads and thousand arms, each one ending in a hand containing an eye, didn't seem so alien. For what better way of representing the all-seeing, all-encompassing nature of a divinity of compassion than with a thousand arms, eyes and heads facing in all directions? Now I understood why Chenrezig held a white lotus, and why the Dalai Lama is also called 'The Holder of the White Lotus', for just as the lotus is born and rises out of mud to burst into exquisite flower, so the human being can rise out of limitation and ignorance to blossom into the sublimity of Buddhahood.

It has been Tenzin Gyatso's particular karma to inherit the Dalai Lama's title in arguably the most precarious phase of its entire history. The absolute ruler of the Land of Snows, kept in splendid near-isolation in the mighty Potala Palace, dubbed the eighth wonder of the world, who grew up without ever having seen a train, plane, television set, electricity, or any other scientific achievement of the 20th century, has of necessity become a thoroughly modern man. His bare arm now reveals a patchwork of vaccination scars, showing that the 14th Dalai Lama has well and truly become a 'citizen of the world', as he now likes to call himself. He dashes around the world, like a Buddhist John Paul II, promoting peace and representing, when and where he is able, the human rights of his people in Tibet, and their struggle for freedom.

The Dalai Lama's personal history reads like something out of a romantic, mystical fairy tale. He was discovered by exactly the same process as his other 13 incarnations. When his predecessor died in the Year of the Water Bird (1933), the search began immediately to find his reincarnation. As they had done for hundreds of years the most eminent sages and meditators within the court of the Dalai Lama began to watch for signs that would indicate the whereabouts of their future god-king. They took note that 'The Great Thirteenth', as he was called, while meditating in the clear light following his 'death', moved his head one night towards the north-east. Next, a star-shaped fungus appeared in the north-east side of the room housing the chorten (mausoleum) built to honour the Dalai Lama who had just passed away. And a dragon-flower suddenly sprang up in the main courtyard of the Potala, also on the north-east side.

The Regent appointed to govern the country until the Dalai Lama was found, then journeyed to the sacred lake of Lhamo Namtso, 90 miles south-east of Lhasa, where adepts had frequently looked into the water to see visions of the future. The story goes that as he looked the wind arose and the blue water turned white. A blue-black hole formed in this white water, above which clouds appeared. Beneath the clouds the Regent then saw a monastery with golden roofs, a twisting road leading to a nearby mountain, and then a small house with distinctive turquoise tiles. In the garden of the house was a peach tree in bloom, and a woman with a baby in her arms. The Regent knew he had seen his future leader.

The search parties duly set out – one to the north-east, the most favoured direction, one to the south and another to the south-east. On their journey to the north-east the search party came across the Kumbum monastery with its distinctive roofs and cupolas of gold and copper glistening in the sun. They rode on further until they reached the village of Takster where they saw a small house with turquoise tiles and a peach tree in bloom. It stood at the end of a long, winding road beneath a mountain. Excitement rose. According to tradition, the high lama leading the party, Keutsang Rinpoche, then changed clothes and position with the lesser official (in order to maintain the secrecy of the mission) and went to the house to see if a young boy-child was inside. The 'lama' was greeted at the front door while his 'servant' was shown into the kitchen where he found a small boy who immediately ran to him with open arms shouting, 'Lama, Lama'. This was doubly exciting because the word for lama in the dialect of the region is 'Aga' – a term the boy by rights should have used. The child was clearly delighted with his visitor, climbed up on his knee and grabbed the mala around Keutsang Rinpoche's neck, given to him long before by the 13th Dalai Lama. 'This is mine,' said the child. The rinpoche said he could have it if he could guess who he was. The child looked at him and said 'Sera Aga' – meaning a lama from Sera monastery in Lhasa, which was exactly where Keutsang Rinpoche had received his education.

The official tests then began. As prospective reincarnated beings have been expected to do over the centuries, the child from Takster was asked to identify his belongings from his previous life – a mala, a drum and a walking stick mixed up with others, some the same, some more attractive. The child chose correctly each time. And so his game of 'riding to Lhasa', which he had played ever since his parents could remember, was enacted in reality. The three-month journey ended when Tenzin Gyatso entered Lhasa riding in a silk-lined palanquin to the delighted cries of his people who lined the streets weeping with joy. He was then placed on the seven-foot-high Lion Throne and crowned the 14th Dalai Lama. He was just four years old.

Today the middle-aged man with the kind face and glasses is, like all reincarnated lamas, reticent about his past lives. The first time I met him, at the end of the interview which was largely political in nature, I asked him if he remembered any of his other previous incarnations. He laughed. 'At the moment, no,' he replied in his rich, musical baritone voice. 'When I was young, around three or four, I did demonstrate quite clearly, I am told, about my past memory. At that time I used to speak a dialect which was not spoken in my birthplace. And, of course, I showed the search party that I knew my previous incarnation.'

Boldly, I probed deeper. Did he remember anything *now*? 'Not much. I have certain mystic experiences – but besides these things I have no memory,' he replied cautiously. I dared press no further. The Dalai Lama clearly did not want to say anything more and I did not want to risk an outright rebuttal, but 'mystic experiences' opened up a mine of possibilities.

In Dharamsala I asked him who he was. 'A stupid human being!

I am just a simple Buddhist monk, that's all,' he laughed. I wasn't going to let him get away with that. 'But people believe you are an embodiment of Chenrezig, the Buddha of Compassion,' I insisted. His Holiness paused, looked very thoughtful and said, 'Ah, you see that is the question of reincarnation. There are different types of reincarnation. From the believer's point of view I do have some special relation to some high beings – that I can say. But still I am just a Buddhist monk. A naughty Buddhist monk. But as far as my motivation is concerned I am quite sincere. I feel I am a sincere person. That's all,' he said. His words were brilliant, revealing everything, and nothing.

Later I read his autobiography, *My Land and My People*, in which he indirectly speaks more extensively on this 'relation to high beings'. 'Buddhas are reincarnated solely to help others, since they themselves have already achieved the highest of all levels. They are not reincarnated through any active volition of their own; such an active mental process has no place in Nirvana. They are reincarnated rather by the innate wish to help others, through which they have achieved Buddhahood. Their reincarnations occur whenever conditions are suitable and do not mean that they leave their state in Nirvana. In simile it is rather as reflections of the moon may be seen on earth in placid lakes and seas when conditions are suitable while the moon itself remains in its course in the sky. By the same simile, the moon may be reflected in many different places at the same moment and a Buddha may incarnate simultaneously in many different bodies. All such incarnate beings, as I already indicated can influence by their own wishes in each life the place and time when they will be reborn and after each birth they have a lingering memory of their previous life which enables others to identify them.'

If he is reluctant to talk about his transcendent powers and his connection with the higher beings, his actions and attitudes reveal in no uncertain terms what a saintly man the Dalai Lama is, whether you believe in reincarnation or not. Having seen thousands of his subjects tortured and killed in the years following the Chinese invasion, his culture demolished, and he himself forced into exile, fleeing one night from his palace dressed as a common soldier and riding on a yak over the highest mountains in the world to India, one might expect him to be a little bitter. Not at all. His attitude towards his oppressors is one of astonishing equanimity.

'They are human beings the same as everyone. They have the same feelings – those of wanting happiness and not wanting suffering. So there is no need to feel hatred or anger,' he said. 'As people who practise the Mahayana Buddhist teaching we pray every day to develop some kind of unlimited altruism. So there is no point in developing hatred for the Chinese. Rather we should develop respect for them, and love and compassion.' Then he added gently, 'We must, however, clarify the Chinese ignorance. That's our aim and moral responsibility. The Chinese have created their own world, their imaginary Tibet. They feel they have come as "liberators". Ultimately they have to realize that it is a separate country. If Tibet was always truly a part of China then, whether Tibetans liked it or not they would have to live with it. But that is not the case,' said the Dalai Lama, who refuses to become militant, much to several of his countrymen's dismay.

But surely, I asked, he must have found the drastic change in his lifestyle somewhat disturbing. He had 'fallen' from a magnificent palace to a modest bungalow, his 'kingdom' was now a hilltop, and his official status that of refugee. Thinking of how the Shah of Iran crumbled, physically and mentally, when he lost his country, did the Dalai Lama not experience any trauma when he left Tibet?

'Oh, no. I didn't find it at all difficult to adjust,' said His Holiness cheerfully. 'In fact I think these different, difficult circumstances have helped a lot. If I had remained in Tibet under the previous system, the same society and conditions, I would not have had to face reality. In other words since I became a refugee, and have experienced tragedy, I have had to face the harsh facts of life. When everything goes smoothly in life you can pretend everything is OK. But when you face a difficult period then there is no way you can pretend. You have to accept reality. And through difficulties you gain more courage, more patience – and that's very important in one's life.'

In fact the Dalai Lama likes to approach much of life with the same down-to-earth practicality, dispelling any fanciful, romantic images people might hold about an incarnate Buddha. He once replied to an open-mouthed BBC interviewer that no, he didn't miss the Potala at all because it really didn't have any decent lavatories! And when I asked him about his hobbies he replied, endearingly, 'I make seedings and bulbings [gardening] and some small mechanics. I carry on some small repair work, mainly watches. I like to repair the little things that go wrong with watches – not the quartz type. Not only my own watches but those of my close acquaintances. Without pay!' he chuckled. 'And then I like reading, history and astronomy. My English vocabulary is not very great but there is a great urge to read science books. My one handicap is my laziness. When I get to a certain word and get stuck, due to my laziness I don't get the dictionary. So I let it go. Previously I very much liked to walk and go mountain climbing – but here again I'm lazy. Too lazy! However, mentally I remain active. There is hardly ever a moment when my mind is not working. That seldom happens. But physically I'm very lazy, I think,' he said, laughter bubbling out from somewhere deep inside him.

With the same devastating honesty he admits that there was much about Tibet that he did not like. 'There were certain cere-monial activities that took up a lot of time but the substance was – not much,' he said candidly. He has also stated that in his opinion Tibetans were too bound by tradition and he himself was kept too remote from his people. He is much happier now than he can wander more freely among them, and most of the mighty trappings of his office have, by necessity, been dropped. So, in a way I was not surprised by his answer to my last question, as to whether he will be the last Dalai Lama, as the ancient prophecy suggests.

'Whether the recognized reincarnated one comes depends on circumstances. My own rebirth and reincarnation will be definite, but whether or not people will recognize the next Dalai Lama depends on what will happen. Sometimes I feel I might be the last Dalai Lama. If there is a usefulness for a Dalai Lama, then naturally people will recognize him. But if there is no usefulness for a Dalai Lama then forget it! Actually I am not that interested in the institution of the Dalai Lama. Tibet's history is long, and the Dalai Lama's history is quite short. Just a few centuries. In fact in the early history before the Dalai Lama came Tibet was more powerful – and since the Dalai Lama it has become more divided. Actually, the Dalai Lama is only about one individual – what is more important is our nation.'

Much to his own people's disquietude the Dalai Lama actually drew up a draft constitution in 1963, including a clause that would allow for his own impeachment. Now he is talking about new methods for electing his successor, maybe in the style of a pope.

The Dalai Lama has met Osel several times now, first in his meditations, then in the flesh together with his family, and later when he personally performed the ritualistic cutting of the hair ceremony, in Dharamsala, signifying Osel's status as a renunciate. He has always taken a keen interest in his welfare and progress. Once for a Spanish television programme on Osel, His Holiness explained in his light, almost jocular manner precisely how he had come to select him as Lama Yeshe's incarnation. 'First I received a list of candidates from Lama Zopa, then I tested, and the Spanish boy won the election. He got the most votes! So I decided – he was the incarnation of the late Lama Yeshe,' he stated in matter-of-fact tones.

That such an occurrence should happen does not surprise him at all, he says. 'Buddhism is somethng new in the West; more people are taking an interest in it, particularly Tibetan Buddhism, maybe because it places more emphasis on reason and the logical process rather than simply on faith, which appeals to some people. It also provides many different methods to practise, understand and meditate, so it has the attraction of the supermarket,' he said. 'So the fact that Lama Yeshe, whose main work was in the West should be born in Spain, seems quite logical. Actually there are quite a few western reincarnated lamas now,' he said.

Indeed Osel is not the first Tibetan lama to be reborn in western form, although he is undoubtedly the most famous and arguably the most eminent to date. But other lamas have appeared in the USA, New Zealand, France and several other western countries and are being quietly nurtured by the western Buddhist communities to whom they are affiliated.

The Dalai Lama expounded in his typically down-to-earth way what to him was the purpose of such reincarnations: 'For certain Dharma work one human life is not sufficient. More time is required to carry on the work started in the previous life. So, in these cases, reincarnation is useful. In other cases where reincarnate lamas merely acquire social status, then the whole process is not so useful,' he added with devastating honesty. He has also stated more than once that an ordinary geshe (doctor of divinity) who taught and lived the religious path diligently was of far more value than a lofty reincarnate who demonstrates little spiritual advancement. 'The main proof of reincarnation should always be demonstrated from the child himself,' he said.

He repeated this message to Maria and Paco when he granted the whole family an audience in Bodhgaya, India, in February 1987, shortly after they had arrived from Spain. He looked sharply at Osel and asked penetrating questions about his behaviour and development. When Maria replied that he was so sensitive that he responded like a chameleon to whatever atmosphere was presented to him, and that his energy was so strong that it was difficult at times to know how to treat him, the Dalai Lama said, 'Relate to Osel like with a normal child, but know in your minds that he is a reincarnated lama. Sometimes you will need to scold him, and if it is necessary spank him, but without ever forgetting who he is. The more naughty they are when they are small, the better they are when they grow up,' he said with a laugh.

He then told them to watch Osel very closely as he starts to speak. 'Very soon Osel will start talking and he will say who he is. We must be very aware of this moment. This moment is very important,' he advised. It was a prophecy that was soon to come true.

He talked about what he envisaged the future to hold for such an unusual and important child. 'He needs education and discipline. When he is four or five years old he will start his studies, and when he is eight he will have to go to the monastery and study in a more serious way. I think maybe Sera [in southern India] will be good for him. He will have to study for at least 10 years and simultaneously he must receive personal teachings from a master, do retreats and develop a strong personal practice. After that, maybe when he is 20 or 25, he will be ready to benefit many beings – mostly in the West.

'Osel will be able to bring together two very important circumstances: to be a westerner, but with the wisdom of the East. Later, he might even go to Tibet to teach and the Tibetans will be amused to see a lama with fair hair and light eyes,' he said laughing. Then, looking intently at Osel, he added, 'Yes, he is full of energy and life. He will be very good.'

If this brilliant but humble man, who claims his true religion is kindness, is the last in the line of Dalai Lamas, then the world will have lost one of its richest and most ancient treasures. But as His Holiness himself is only too aware, our times are rapidly changing, and monks must come down from the mountain, mingle with the masses and help them to rise a little above the gross materialism that is now our universal creed. In that process the face of Buddhism itself must inevitably change, evolving to meet the demands of the time. Being the most fluid of all religions, dealing as it does with the state of man's mind, it's a job that is not beyond its capabilities. And it's a task that Lama Yeshe, that most far-sighted and broad-minded of men, saw way ahead of his time, and began to implement. He was hindered by his health and his traditional roots that lay buried deep in the past. Lama Osel, however, as his reincarnation, is young, fresh and western. What better figure to lead the way to the new Buddhism?

16

LAMA OSEL

Now, a year on from the enthronement, I find myself back at Kopan, that magical hill in the middle of the Kathmandu valley, writing the account of all that I have known and understood about the extraordinary story of Lama Yeshe, who moved so many hearts, and the Spanish child who is said to be his reincarnation. Like all my decisions to fly to this Buddhist monastery, this one came on the spur of the moment and, like all the rest, has somehow proved exactly right. Where better to recall and set down all that has happened in these past years than the place where it all started?

My situation has improved considerably since I first came here in 1976. I no longer roll out my sleeping bag in a cramped room with eight other women, nor on a wooden bed in a small concrete cell. Now I sit in my own three-roomed house with its wide arches, stone fireplace in the corner, double bedroom, complete with foam mattress, sheets and blankets – and the acme of luxury, a flushing loo. The house sits half-way down the hill but is still well within the monastery compound. I am surrounded by groves of mango trees, the constant call of exotic birds, and through my windows I can see the women in their brightly coloured longhis working the terraced fields, the great Stupa of Boudhanath with the Buddha eyes beneath its summit surveying the four directions, and beyond that the towering mauve and purple ranges of the Himalayas with the constant play of clouds around those mighty peaks.

It's a simple, healthy life, far removed from my Chelsea existence. My sink is still a cold stand-pipe outside my front door where, along with the local farmer's wife, I wash my plates and few clothes. My 'bath' is still a bucket, but now that I've come here in spring the cold douche is very welcome. I eat with the community – plain nourishing vegetarian fare – the main meal still being served at 11.30 a.m. I am happy here.

Lama Osel is three years old now, beginning to speak both English and Spanish fluently, and lives in Lama Yeshe's former rooms in the main Gompa at the top of the hill. He is clearly perfectly at home. Everything had to change in order for everything to stay the same.

He has been here for just over a year now. In the weeks that I have been here I have been able to piece together the events since I last saw him. After his enthronement in Dharamsala, his destiny slowly but inexorably began to take shape. When all the reporters and cameramen had scurried away with their stories and the ex-students of Lama Yeshe had returned to their own countries to ponder on the meaning of what had taken place, Osel quietly made his way back to his former home, Nepal, and took up the threads of his former life in earnest. His babyhood was at an end. From now on he was to be separated from Paco, his father and constant companion for the two short years of his life, and handed over to the care of Gloria Mallol, a 50-year-old Spanish nun. Gloria, a small dark woman from Barcelona, had known Osel since he was seven days old and had travelled with the Hita Torres family on their exodus from Spain to India. The parting from Paco in Dharamsala had hurt, but not for long. Once the situation had been explained to him, the tears had dried, never to return. It is always like that with him. He only needs to be given an explanation for his mind, and mood, to change instantly.

And so he journeyed back to Kopan, the place where it had all started, and his family followed behind him. They lived not very far away, in the house where I am now staying, and saw him daily. Paco built a swing for him under the mango tree and every afternoon Osel would arrive with Gloria to play with his siblings. But although they were physically still close, in reality their worlds were drifting further and further apart.

Osel now lived under the regime of all tulkus (reincarnated lamas). He slept not in a cot, but in the carved wooden bed belonging to Lama Yeshe, while his attendant stretched out on the floor on a mattress beside him. There were rules which everyone had to honour. No one was to lean over him, or touch him unnecessarily, especially the crown of his head. He was to eat only from his own plate, drink only from his own cup and use only his own cutlery – which all had to be washed and dried separately.

He had his own linen and towels, and if he visited another household no cloth or blanket was to be used to cover his body that did not belong to him. More specifically he wasn't to be cuddled or kissed, unless he initiated it, for whereas Osel could cuddle and kiss as much as he liked he was not to be the focus for anyone else's emotional or physical needs, including his mother's.

And so no one was to forget who they had in their midst at any time. Osel, although only a toddler, had to be treated with all the deference due to a fully grown spiritual master. As one Tibetan explained to me, 'We treat our tulkus with all the special care and attention that you in the West give to highly contagious people, only with us it's the other way round – we isolate our tulkus as much as possible to prevent them from becoming contaminated from us! You see we believe they are so pure that they can be harmed from coming into too close a contact from us.' In fact Tibetans take their respect much further than any westerner – standing up whenever a baby tulku comes into the room, making sure their seat is always lower than his, and ensuring they always walk behind.

So Lama Zopa, when he gave Gloria her instructions, admonished, 'Lama Osel is more precious than anyone can imagine. We must all relate to him in a special way.' For Gloria the responsibility was huge. Even though she liked young children and used to look after her four younger brothers, she had no experience of being in charge of an incarnate lama, especially the one of her own former guru. Ironically Gloria had met Lama Yeshe on Ibiza, along with Paco, Maria and the next attendant of his reincarnation, Spanish monk Basili Llorca. The job was made more difficult because Gloria had always been rather nervous in front of Lama Yeshe. 'I always felt he was so great, and I was nothing, although he was always very kind to me,' she told me in the little hut perched right at the top of Kopan hill where she now spends most of her time in retreat.

In fact it was Lama Yeshe who sent Gloria to Osel-Ling, maybe to wait for him to be reborn there. 'Just before he died he called me to him and said, "Now you are going to look after my things." I didn't know what he meant. His words then made no sense to me at all. Now I think he planned the whole thing. Lama Osel needed a woman, a mature Spanish woman to look after him when he first came to Kopan – the "mother energy" was more important at that stage, when he was only two, than the male,' said Gloria, who stayed with Osel constantly for a year before she handed him over to Basili's care, and the world of masculine monasticism.

In that time of constant communion she got to know the little lama extremely well. It was, she says, a complete learning experience. 'He made me free. Free from all expectations. My relationship with him was not like that with a child. It was completely different – deep in a way it is impossible to describe. When Lama Osel looks at you he looks right into your eyes, into your very being. Children do not look at you like that – they are not that interested in people in that way. But Lama Osel looks right into you and relates with what he finds. And so he has a different way of behaving with each person. I know that with me he completely mirrored my mind,' explained Gloria, sitting on her meditation cushion in her tiny house while I propped myself up on her bed.

'I remember once he would not go to sleep and so I scolded him. That didn't do any good so I began to sing. He liked that and so I kept singing for an hour, but he still wouldn't sleep. I got cross and then upset. Lama Osel looked at me then and smiled as though to say, "This is all empty – you don't believe any of this really.", closed his eyes and promptly fell asleep. It was sometimes as though this body, this business of being a baby, then a child, is all a game to him – something he has to go through. When he was crying I used to say to him, "What are you doing?" – and he'd stop instantly and begin to imitate himself. "Boo, hoo, hoo," he'd say with a grin, not taking himself seriously. It is as if there were no ego there.'

She had many insights into this child-man which utterly convinced her that he was Lama Yeshe come back. 'He couldn't bear suffering. If he saw someone was sick, or heard a child crying he wanted to go to them right away. More than that, he wanted to do something. He would try to blow on the cut or hurt part of the body, trying to make it better, the way Tibetan lamas do. His physical skill is exceptional too. He has complete control over all his actions which to me indicates he has complete control over his mind. He is incredibly tidy and precise. He never knocks anything over but handles everything with supreme care. For example when he was two he could serve tea, pouring the milk into the cup, adding the sugar and lifting the teapot to pour the tea without spilling anything. This kind of precision I found amazing. He has enormous powers of concentration. When he is interested in something, he goes deeply into the experience of it, everything around him disappears and nothing can distract him. It shows when he's playing with something, or when he's watching television. He loves TV just like Lama Yeshe, but the interesting thing is ever since he was very little he can watch it for hours at a time. His older sister, Dolma, could never sit for two hours engrossed in any programme, but Lama Osel watches without moving.'

To Gloria, Lama Osel's mind is indisputably powerful but she still believes it needs to be developed. Lama Zopa had told her: 'Lama Osel's mind is already in the nature of clear light but this mind needs to be brought forth. What is inside needs to be brought to the outside. Lama did not need to be reborn – he came only for our sakes, only to please us. He will become whatever we want. If we want a lama we have to build one – if we want an object of enjoyment, that is what we will get.' Gloria agrees. 'These high lamas come back but still have to go through the whole learning process. They learn fast but they need our help. We have to teach them and we have to teach them well,' she said.

It was with this in mind that Gloria would smack her charge whenever he did not listen to reason. For along with all the rules about treating Osel as though he were a precious gem Lama Zopa had also instructed Gloria to correct him if he were naughty. Gloria, strict but kind, had carried out Lama Zopa's orders to the letter. 'I never hit him with anger – that's the point – and afterwards he always hugged me. He has a very strong personality, but he is also very sweet. He never liked me being displeased with him and when he realized he had done something wrong was always contrite. Usually there was no need to smack him. I would just have to tell him to stop and he would. He's a very humble person – very soft. He is easy to teach. To me he really has no faults, he is entirely pure,' she said.

The liaison between the child and the Spanish nun was further cemented when Gloria accompanied Osel on his three-month tour of Australia and New Zealand, where with Lama Zopa they visited all the centres which Lama Yeshe had founded. If Gloria was to find herself exhausted by the full itinerary and constant travelling, Osel was in his element. Whenever he could he broke free from Gloria's clutches to make contact with complete strangers who were obviously captivated by the little boy in the Tibetan Buddhist robes. On the way to Australia he entertained the entire plane with his antics – not that Gloria could see what he was doing, she merely heard the roars of laughter coming from the seats behind her. He played sand-castles with people he met on the beach, held hands with mothers he found in the playground, and joined couples in restaurants, insisting his food be brought to their table so that he could eat with them. Osel, the extrovert, was going walkabout, reaching out to people – just like Lama Yeshe had done in Australia, when he put on shorts and a big hat to see how ordinary western people lived their lives.

One woman who came off the same plane as Osel was heard to say to the girl who met her, 'I don't know who that child is, but he is unlike any child I've ever met before. His presence is absolutely remarkable.'

As on his previous tours to the USA and Europe, Osel was perfectly at home in the various FPMT centres, seeming to know automatically who was the main person in charge and making a special effort to pay attention to them. 'He would single them out, play with them more, stroke their arm, pull their ear in a gesture of affection as though thanking them for all their kindness and hard work. Wherever he went he was always comfortable, relaxed. It was as if he knew this was family. He certainly wasn't at all thrown by all the changes of location and faces, which is strange for a child of that age.'

In Chenrezig Institute, in Eudlo, Queensland, the first of the FPMT centres, Osel gave his first teachings. He gathered around him the children of the families who had come to see him and began teaching them the mantra of Manjushri – the Buddha of Wisdom – saying it over and over again, and waiting for the children to repeat it back to him. He obviously enjoyed his task, entering into it with great enthusiasm and enjoyment. In New Zealand he startled more people by getting hold of a religious text and pretending to 'read' it to the goats in the field outside. He climbed up on a wooden fence, leant over, and with his face just a few feet from his hairy congregation began to 'read' the spiritual message of the famous 'Heart Sutra', the Buddha's profound treatise on Emptiness. Like Lama Yeshe, Osel was beginning to reveal a prodigious love and concern for all animals. On this tour he showed surprisingly little fear of all the strange and large animals he met. One photograph has captured him sitting in a compound of very large kangaroos, alone and completely at ease.

The close of the Australian and New Zealand tour also marked the end of Gloria's time as official attendant to Osel. When they returned to Kopan she relinquished her position to the Spanish monk, Basili Llorca. The separation was exceedingly painful for her. 'I had become very attached to him,' she said. Osel, however, took the change in his stride. 'Perhaps that is the most amazing thing about him. If he were not a special person he would be completely crazy by now, having had so many people looking after him and then having to leave them. He cares very much for the person who is with him – be it Paco, or me or his mother or Lama Zopa – but he is not attached. When it is time to part he does not mind. It was much harder for me to say goodbye than for him,' said Gloria.

At the same time Maria, Paco and the other Hita Torres children were also being put through their own particular paces. While Osel was easily adapting to his new, globe-trotting, independent life, his blood family who had valiantly uprooted themselves to follow their youngest member to Nepal were finding their new existence not quite the romantic adventure it may have seemed back in the quiet mountains of Bubión.

'At first it was *very* difficult,' Maria confessed. 'We had all the trauma of packing up and moving and not being sure of where we were going – whether it was Dharamsala or Nepal. Everything was new for us, and everything uncertain. The children became very insecure and unsettled. I was insecure as well. I didn't know what the future would bring, what we were doing. On top of all that I discovered I was pregnant again (once more in spite of contraception!) and that made me doubly sensitive.'

After the enthronement they too found their way to Kopan but that did not solve all their problems. Life on the beautiful peaceful hill, with its trees, bushes and animals was a perfect playground for the children. Furthermore they were near Osel and were treated with the respect and kindness due to the family of the reincarnated founder of the monastery. But on a practical level things were far from right. The house was exceedingly small for so large a family, it didn't have a proper kitchen, there was no hot water and all the children had to sleep in one room. They didn't like the food prepared by the monastery and one by one they succumbed to diarrhoea, the most common affliction in Nepal.

'It was clear they needed to go to a proper school, not only for their education but to make friends and get some outside interest. We'd found one Spanish teacher in Kopan but that wasn't enough. Their energy needed to be channelled into something more structured – to stop them fighting between themselves. But I didn't know what to do. The only schools here were either Nepali or the International school, and my children could only speak Spanish. It was a very bad situation, and I became quite depressed. The monsoon was coming, to make matters worse, as the children would then be stuck inside all day. We had no money – and then Paco went off to Tibet with Lama Zopa, leaving me alone and pregnant to cope with the situation.'

Being a woman of courage and strength, Maria decided to take matters into her own hands. While Paco was still away in Tibet she decided the only sensible course of action was to leave the confines of Kopan, move into a bigger house in Kathmandu and put the children into the American International School. The decision to leave Osel was difficult but necessary. Their worlds were drifting further and further apart.

'I didn't want to leave Osel but I could see he was happy and very healthy, while my four other children were not. They became my main priority – I had a big responsibility towards them too. They were unsettled and insecure. I needed to create a proper home and start giving them a good diet to clear up their stomach problems. I did miss Osel a little at first, but quite honestly I was too preoccupied with my other children's needs and my pregnancy to be worried about him. I made a special room for him and Basili in the house I found, and he came to stay with us for a few days at a time, and then once or twice a week. It was fine,' she said.

The children went to the American school on 27 August and Maria gave birth on 3 September – at home, with Paco, a nurse from Kopan and a Spanish au pair to help her. It was another easy, pain-free delivery and the baby, named Kunkyen (meaning 'Omniscience') by Lama Zopa is already showing signs of being another special child. 'We have been told he may be another lama, but that observations will not be done until later,' said Maria who has now become almost used to the idea of mothering holy beings. 'I suppose we are now an ideal family for high lamas to take birth into – we live in auspicious places, near Tibetan monasteries, we have connections with Tibetan lamas, and there is already one recognized lama amongst us to pave the way. When I said to Lama Zopa that I really didn't want to have any more children he replied, "If they are special, why not?" At least my children do not damage me in any way,' said Maria who, in spite of bearing and breast-feeding six children, still has the figure of a 20-year-old girl.

It was in the midst of all these major life-changes that Maria and Paco were informed that Lama Zopa wanted Osel to go to Australia. Although they were now physically separated from Osel, and had mentally prepared themselves for the independent life they knew he would have to make, the news was a bombshell. The thought of him being in a different continent shook them more than they ever thought possible. This, they knew, was finally the reality of having the reincarnation of Lama Yeshe as their son.

'We were both very upset, Paco even more than me. I could understand intellectually the reasons for him having to go but I was still not happy. To be honest I was already uneasy about Gloria being with him all the time and thought that after three months away with her he would be more attached to her than me. I thought he might not even recognize me when he got back. I didn't like the idea at all,' said Maria honestly. They'd received the message from Lama Zopa, who was already travelling, via a lot of people, and decided that if he really thought Osel should go to Australia and New Zealand, he should let them know himself. Without further ado Lama Zopa got on the telephone to Maria and Paco and asked them if they would kindly let their son go. For Maria it was a turning-point. 'I then accepted the proposal completely. I remembered how beneficial it was for the people in America and Europe to see Lama Osel – and knew it would be good for the people in Australia and New Zealand to see the living proof of reincarnation too. They needed to see Osel. I also realized how much Osel would enjoy being with Lama Zopa for that length of time. So I understood there weren't any "bad" reasons why Osel shouldn't go on this tour – only my attachment. I tried to explain all this to Paco, but he was still very emotional about it. When we went together – Paco, Osel and me – to get the visa for Osel to enter Australia we had to sign a document giving permission for Osel to travel without us. That was the beginning of my knowing what renunciation truly is,' said Maria.

But a strange thing happened at the last minute which completely changed Maria and Paco's mind. They went to the airport with Maria's parents, who were visiting them, and a crowd of Lama Yeshe's students to see Osel off. Osel was relaxed and played with the children, like the 2½-year-old he was. When the time came for him to go he suddenly changed. 'He stopped being our child and became a lama – blessing us, giving us katags. We were no longer his family, we became "sentient beings", the same as everyone else around. He put his hands together and said "bye-bye" kindly to us all. He waved as he walked away, hand in hand with Gloria. My father, who is agnostic, was utterly amazed. "I don't know who this child is, but he is not ordinary," he said.

'After that Paco and I became very quiet. Osel had not singled us out for any special treatment when he left. He obviously did not need us. Paco could see there was no reason for him to be upset. That night alone we talked about it. What we had done we knew was for the best. We offered our son to give happiness to the Australian and New Zealand people. That was the moment of our real renunciation. I understood then, that Lama Osel is a treasure we have in our hearts, a treasure that cannot be stolen or lost. We will have it all our lives.'

When he returned, however, Osel recognized his parents immediately, happy to see them again. He took their hands and began to speak in both Spanish and English. Maria and Paco realized what strides he had made in the months he'd been away. He came to live with them for three days and they had an Australian boy over to play with him. 'Be careful, he's a little lama,' said the boy's mother. 'No, a big lama,' joked Osel. The sophistication, as well as the language, was rapidly developing.

Maria and Paco now see Osel once a week when he visits them (although Paco frequently rides up to Kopan on his motor bike to see his son when the mood takes him) and they are happy with that.

'It's enough. We make Sunday a special day, preparing a nice lunch, telling stories, devoting the whole day to the children. If Lama Osel didn't come down, it would be a day like any other, so now we all have a nice time. We still have a special relationship with Osel, he's still our son, and we are still his parents. Most of all we know he's happy in Kopan,' they say.

Maria is now so happy with the way things have worked out

that she says she will willingly give Kunkyen to Lama Zopa if he too turns out to be another incarnate lama. I asked her once where she got her unusual, detached attitude towards her children from.

'I do not know,' she replied. 'But with all my children I believed the golden rule was to give them space to discover the world for themselves, to create their own vision of life, not their parents'. Most women have children out of need, out of attachment, and then they create a relationship of need with the children, so that if they are separated neither the mother nor child can stand it. That has never been my way. I wanted to give my children freedom. That, I think, is real love. All of them can live apart from Paco and me without any distress. It does not mean you love them less because you let them go. You love them more,' she said.

And then I remembered Lama Yeshe's comment to an American woman, Marietta, some time before he died. 'Maria has exactly the qualities I would like in a mother,' he had said.

To date, life for the Hita Torres family is working out well, although Paco, who still speaks little English, finds himself lonely from time to time, and sometimes wishes he could return to Spain. 'Everything has happened very fast – sometimes I feel as though I am caught up in events which are overtaking me,' said the shy, reserved man who is less gregarious than his wife. 'But I trust Lama Zopa, and am still willing to do whatever he suggests,' he told me.

The children are still happy at the American school, and Maria has found a way of paying the enormous fees. She takes bundles of exquisite hand-painted silk dresses to Spain and sells them. Her business acumen is as sharp as ever it was when she was selling stamps long before this adventure began. 'This is a story of love, compassion, the miracle of the mind and hope. People want to hear these things. They are tired by all the negativity in the world today, all the bad news. I receive letters from people all over the world congratulating me and saying how lucky I am. People who are not Buddhists. They write asking me to give their love to Osel and saying they hope they will be lucky enough to meet him in the future,' she said.

She was right. In the dreariness, and sometimes blackness, of our humdrum lives, the story of Osel had indeed become an event of love and hope.

17

NOW

For three months now I have sat on Kopan Hill and watched Osel, the boy lama, go about his daily business. It has been both a pleasure and a privilege, for the days when one can simply walk up the winding stone steps beside the Gompa, enter his rooms without knocking and play with him to your heart's content are numbered. His time of absolute freedom is coming to an end. Duty and discipline beckon – the destiny he was born to.

And so for this short period I have looked with fascination and delight at the strong, sturdy little figure toddling around his domain in his maroon skirts held up by yellow braces, the silver protection locket from Lama Zopa constantly around his neck, the yellow base-ball hat protecting his shaved head from the searing rays of the Nepali summer sun. Wherever he goes he brings smiles. 'You see,' says Lama Zopa, 'he is already bringing happiness to so many people, just by his presence.' And so he goes about, patting the huge Kopan dogs, playing in the sand-pit, a self-contained, composed little boy with an aura of deep contentment about him. For the most part he appears serious and thoughtful, although the vitality is ever-present, and the sense of humour never far beneath the surface.

He has his moments of childishness when he cries because he cannot have his way, but they are rare and short-lived. Osel mostly doesn't seem like a child at all – rather an adult living in a child's body, going through the motions of childlike behaviour because that is what is expected of him. He seems curiously in command of all situations. '*Not* "Lama", Tenzin Osel,' were the first words he addressed to me, quietly but firmly, on my day of arrival. 'My name, Tenzin Osel,' he repeated. I listened, noting that perhaps he was not only telling me he had received the extra name 'Tenzin' from the Dalai Lama recently (when His Holiness also cut his hair and welcomed him into monastic life) but that he was making a distinction between himself and Lama Yeshe or 'Lama', the name by which everyone calls him. Tenzin Osel clearly wanted me to know he had his own identity.

He comes to see me quite often. He stands in my room watching me type, looking at me with a disarmingly steady gaze. I tell him where I am up to, and he listens intently. He understands everything I say and, I feel, much, much more.

It constantly amazes me that in spite of all the attention focused upon him he isn't spoilt. It could so easily have happened, what with the constant flow of journalists, cameramen, TV crews, the prostrations, presents and devoted students ready to do his bidding. That he isn't seems partly to do with his own nature and with the kind, firm hand of Basili Llorca, his attendant.

'I wouldn't like to see him indulged – as can happen with some other rinpoches who are given Rolexes and other expensive gifts. The best thing I can do, I feel, is humbly to help him manifest the inner qualities of a lama such as humility, generosity, detachment, kindness. If he is a lama of great worth it must come from his side – I'm going to do my best not to let him be conditioned,' said Basili, who like Gloria, his first attendant, is not averse to giving Osel what he calls 'pam pam' on the bottom when it's needed. The bond between them is obviously strong.

And so for now he lives with Basili, who speaks to him in Spanish, and an Australian monk, David Marks, who speaks to him in English, in the rooms formerly occupied by his previous incarnation: a small bedroom overlooking the front gardens of the Gompa, an even smaller playroom, and a communal dining-room. Around him are the lamas and geshes who came to Kopan inspired by Lama Yeshe and his bold, big vision of bringing Buddha Dharma to the 'injis' (westerners). Their rooms also lead on to the dining-room and general living area. It's a relaxed, informal way of living, Tibetan-style, each person keeping to his or her own quarters but sharing the main living space.

His day is simple and each one follows much the same pattern. He rises at 7.30 a.m., smiling and in a good mood, according to Basili who sleeps on the floor beside him, and jumps on Basili's shoulders if he has not finished his morning meditations. He then dresses and goes into the playroom for breakfast – porridge, toast and milk, which he eats faster than Basili. Then he does his morning 'pre-school', counting and drawing exercises to develop his motor ability. After that starts the serious business of the day – play. Osel enters into the spirit of play with a dedication and concentration that is indeed worthy of a high lama. He can play for hours on end with his Lego, his trucks and jeeps making up imaginary games which tire all those commandeered into playing with him (be they small monks, large monks or western students) much quicker than they tire him. In the morning he plays indoors, but after lunch, which he eats with his attendants and the resident lamas, he goes outside and continues to play there.

In the afternoon Osel receives visitors – people who have travelled to Kopan to see him and get his blessing, and the press. He usually carries out his obligations well, giving katags to those who come and bow before him, placing his hand on their heads – and dealing with the press like the old pro he is. Cameras still or moving, do not faze him. He poses with aplomb and patience, but when he's had enough will say authoritatively, 'Finish now' and walk away. The press are hardly disappointed. Osel is still excellent copy. Basili, David and the rest of the monastic community have learnt to deal with this public incursion into their lives with equanimity. They know the world's interest in Osel is an ongoing situation and part of Osel's function in this lifetime.

Supper is at 6 p.m. and bed at 7.30 p.m. when Basili reads him a story – his favourite is about a child (who he identifies as 'Osel') travelling on an aeroplane. Basili then stays with him until he goes to sleep.

It is clear that the little Spanish lama is secure in his life in a Buddhist monastery. The same emotional detachment he demonstrated when leaving his family for his Australian tour last year, is still present. He never shows any sign of missing them during the six days he does not see them, although on the Sundays when I have accompanied him to the big house in Kathmandu he clearly enjoys seeing them all. He plays with his siblings and pays particular attention to the baby Kunkyen, who he adores, fetching him water to drink and offering him pieces of fruit through the day, as though serving him. He fits easily into the family routine, but when it is time to go he happily takes Basili's hand, heads straight for the jeep without any fuss, climbs in, gives Maria and Paco a quick blessing, waves goodbye and leaves. It seems almost as though he's had enough and is glad to get back to the peace of the monastery.

'We still need him much more than he needs us,' says Maria. And you can see it is true. I once watched Maria arrive at Kopan after a two-month absence – selling clothes in Spain. She came directly from the airport to see Osel, before going home to spend the rest of the time with her other children. Osel greeted her warmly but not with undue attention. He certainly didn't cling to her, like most children would who'd been separated from their mother for so long. And when it was time for her to go, he was so engrossed in his sand-pit that David had to coax him to stop playing to say goodbye. He let David lift him to see his mother off in the jeep, shut the door for her and said 'goodbye'. As the jeep drove off he ran after it, watching it go down the hill, and when it was out of sight he turned round and, with a smile, took David's hand and calmly walked back into the monastery. 'No, this is not usual behaviour,' agrees Basili, 'but then he is an unusual person.' So, I assume Osel has achieved that state of non-attachment, that freedom from emotional needs and ties which, the Buddhists say, hold us back on the spiritual path because they prevent us from loving truly – freely and unconditionally.

This is not to say that Osel is devoid of warmth and human feelings. On the contrary I have seen him show a concern for people, especially if he thinks they are sick, quite astonishing in a child of his age. He enquires into the nature of bruises, asks what's behind plasters, peers into cuts and sores. He once saw my leg full of mosquito bites and hurriedly led me into his bedroom where his insect repellent cream was, and with small but deft fingers personally anointed each one. He talks a lot about 'pupa', his universal word for anything connoting pain or sickness, pointing out animals in his picture books which 'pupa' and those that do not. He is also worried about animals that are killed for food. 'Cutting death?' he asks, pointing to a cow or chicken wandering across a Kathmandu road, anxious in case the big knives he's seen carving up carcasses by the roadside are meant for the animal in question.

And so I, along with all those who surround Osel, watch and try to fathom out the mystery that has been presented to us – the living example of reincarnation. As for scientific proof I realize there is, and possibly can be, none. One could never produce concrete evidence to demonstrate that the mind-stream of Lama Yeshe had manifested anew in Osel Hita Torres. But neither can one prove conclusively that it has not. If science can show conclusively that the mind (or consciousness) does not exist independently of the brain, or any other part of our fleshly body, then we will know that the doctrine of reincarnation is not true. If this is so, then, according to Buddhist law, it must be rejected, for truth must be honoured above all things.

For all this, I see so many of Lama Yeshe's qualities repeated in Lama Osel that are persuasive, if not conclusive, evidence. These qualities are re-enacted so often they cannot be dismissed as sheer coincidence.

Primarily he is a great communicator, reaching out, extrovert, gregarious. 'Come! Come and play!' he calls to anyone who is passing, inviting them to spend hours with him in his sand-pit or playing with his Lego box. He loves feeding people, handing them cakes and cups of tea. One of his favourite games is cooking imaginary meals – invariably several courses – for the many people he pictures around him, taking real delight in thinking up the ingredients, preparing them and putting them in the pot. Inevitably one's mind flashes back to Lama Yeshe, the prime nurturer.

Now that he is beginning to speak both English and Spanish more fluently it's becoming increasingly clear that communication and communication skills are something he's keenly aware of. He's eager to find and pronounce the right word in the appropriate language, and will repeat new words to himself until he has committed them to memory. Interestingly, he has an unerring memory as to people's nationality, whether Spanish- or English-speaking, and will switch easily from one tongue to the next according to whom he is addressing. There have been some minor attempts to teach him Tibetan – a language he must master if he is to study the texts and learn to debate – but so far they have met with resistance. It seems that, for now, mastering two languages is all he is willing to handle.

He is also like Lama Yeshe in that he likes people to be comfortable and happy, and tries in his small way to make them feel relaxed. Already he's a dab hand at the art of conversation, and performs social gestures as though trying to make you feel welcome. Once when I had returned from a day's shopping in Kathmandu, exhausted by the noise, heat and dust, Osel called me from his bedroom window to come and see him. He told me what he'd had for supper and asked if I had eaten. When I replied that

I had not he produced a box of cheese triangles and enquired whether I would like one. He spent the next three minutes delicately unwrapping the complicated tin foil, refusing all help from me: 'No, I do, you eat,' he insisted. The giving, the caring was once again so reminiscent of Lama.

This kindness, unusual in a small child, extends to small things. He will never refuse anyone anything outright, and rather than say 'No', he will say 'Tomorrow'. He clearly doesn't want to offend or hurt anyone's feelings. If another child takes the car he's playing with, he will take it back, and then go and get another one for the child. '*This* yours,' he will say kindly. I once saw an older monk tease him by pretending to take his new pair of flip-flops. 'These are mine,' said the older monk. 'No, mine!' said Osel, looking worried. 'I like them, and I want them,' teased the monk. Osel thought long and hard about it. 'OK – I take yours,' was the clever but magnanimous answer.

He's kind to his parents, too. 'Osel never wants to give me any trouble, he tries to please,' says Maria. 'For instance if I scold Yeshe for not eating his lunch, Osel will listen without saying anything, and when I have gone into the kitchen he will get down off his chair, go round to Yeshe and try to feed him, even though he is only three and Yeshe nine. And if Lobsang has been naughty and upset me, he will try to spank him. It is endearing.'

There are other more subtle but constant mementoes of Lama Yeshe. Osel's energy is so strong and life-affirming that whenever he walks into a room he fills it. His physical strength, his body which, day by day, is looking more like Lama's – round, solid, sure. And although he hasn't yet astounded anyone with profound Buddhist teachings he still has a sense of who he is. For all his friendliness, he doesn't like overt familiarity. One nun who picked him up to look out of the window and stayed with her arms around him received a quizzical look. 'Too close,' he said, brushing her away gently with his hand – reminding her of the propriety of things. Anyone who oversteps the boundaries and forgets the respect due to a high lama is similarly met with a harsh look of rebuke, or simply ignored.

Osel knows his position, whether it's sitting on the throne, the subject of a puja, or knowing how to deal with his attendants. When David Marks arrived, he brought a present with him. Osel was having breakfast at the time. He watched David prostrate before him and then took the beautifully wrapped gift, but did not open it, like any other child would. Instead he silently handed it to Basili. Only when he'd finished breakfast did he ask Basili to give him the gift. He then carefully undid the string and paper, and smiled with pleasure when he saw that it was a book. He took it to David, sat in his lap, and turned over the pages with him. It was the most gracious acceptance of a gift I had ever seen.

Nevertheless, for all my own growing conviction that Lama Osel is indubitably connected to Lama Yeshe in some way, others who are close to him, like Basili and David, remain wary about stating categorically that he is Lama Yeshe's reincarnation.

'I think he's a special child, for sure. He's very clever and has an excellent memory. He also has a strong personality, and his own views. He knows his own mind, and is extremely determined, but is also very kind and cares deeply about the suffering of others. He has a big sense of humour, too, and is able stand above a situation and laugh. I'm very fond of him, although I hope I'm not attached. And I do see he's making a lot of people happy already and inspiring them. He's got the whole Spanish nation, a Catholic country, thinking about reincarnation for one thing! Somehow he's started his work. I take notice of what Lama Zopa and the Dalai Lama say, and I try to stay open and receptive,' said Basili.

'Still I can't say I believe, and I can't say I don't believe,' he continued. 'To me Lama Yeshe doesn't mean this boy, this body. Lama was a great man, a communicator of wisdom, who reflected the best part of people back on to themselves. These clever things Osel is doing are for me irrelevant. They're entertainment really, and we have enough entertainers on television. From my humble point of view, when Osel becomes a lama, and starts igniting our inner wisdom, then I will recognize his greatness. I feel my job is to help bring that wisdom out.'

No doubt the debate will continue for many years, which is no bad thing – questioning being an essential part of understanding within Tibetan Buddhism. Maybe as he grows up and begins to speak more lucidly he will begin to solve the riddle himself and tell us who he is, and where he comes from, as the Dalai Lama suggests. Already in his baby language he is giving out clues. The other day he was showing me a painting of some Tibetan figures. 'Are they

Buddhas?' I asked. 'No, rinpoches,' replied Osel definitely. 'You too are a rinpoche,' I said. 'No, no,' refuted Osel, laughing. 'But your name is Lama Tenzin Osel Rinpoche,' I pressed. He became quite agitated. 'No, no. Not Rinpoche. Tenzin Osel,' he insisted.

And I remembered his opening words to me, which were also about his identity. The distinction between Lama Yeshe and Lama Osel is important. Osel is *not* Lama Yeshe – we will never see, hear, touch the figure who was Lama Yeshe, but we do have Lama Osel, who is a continuation of the mind of Lama Yeshe but with his own persona. The name itself is significant too. It's a different name, as Osel is quick to point out. But at the deepest level a name is a 'mere label' – it has no absolute reality. And the mind flashes back to that last talk of Lama Yeshe, yet again, saying, 'Am I this body, this name?'

In those months of being with Osel I realized that in a subtle way he had given me hope – a meaning to life that went beyond the mundane everyday values. He had shown me that there was something more than the 'getting and spending', because there is a continuity of lives, and what we do today has a consequence for what we are tomorrow. And surely there is nothing more uplifting than manifest goodness. Lama Yeshe had it; now the hope lies with Lama Osel. Perhaps in all this world of impermanence there is something constant, after all.

The hope is there also that Osel will be the one able to go beyond the literal translation of Tibetan Buddhism and give it to us in our own language, endowed with our own cultural and mental references. The old Tibet has gone, as the recent political unrest has demonstrated, and the butter lamp in front of those ancient Buddha statues is flickering out. But the treasure the Land of Snows held, its priceless wisdom, has escaped and come to us in the West. It will be in a new form. Osel is, I believe, a forerunner of the movement. He will give us Buddhism, 'western-style', as Lama Yeshe so often advocated.

And as his ability to use language improves he will, as Lama Zopa predicted, say more and more things that will amaze us. He is already beginning. The other day when he was alone with Maria he began to talk about his last life. He told her he had a nice car in America. 'Yes?' said Maria intrigued. 'And what colour was it?' she asked, pressing for proof. Silence. Osel couldn't say. 'Red?' she asked, knowing it was his favourite colour, trying to help him. 'No,' he replied definitely. Then, looking round the bathroom where he was, he suddenly saw the taps. '*That* colour,' he said, relieved to have found the means to express what he was trying to convey. Maria knew he was right. Lama Yeshe had indeed a silver car which he used to drive in California.

She then asked him what had happened to Lama Yeshe. 'Lama Yeshe pupa, pupa, pupa,' he said, patting various parts of his body with a pained expression on his face. 'Afterwards, cutting death,' he said, flopping his entire body over sideways, in the pose of someone who had just died. Amazed by the revelations coming voluntarily from her son's mouth, she asked where Lama Yeshe was now. 'Lama Yeshe small, small, playing all the time. Then growing, growing – big,' he added enthusiastically.

Excited by the importance of what Maria had just told me, I took my courage in both hands and, just before I left Kopan, decided to confront Osel myself. The moment was quiet, relaxed, informal. We were alone at the family house, in the bedroom with the baby. 'Kunkyen has hair,' remarked Osel, lifting up the baby's darkening locks. 'Where's your hair?' I joked with Osel, who loves having his head shaved. 'Gone,' he replied with a grin, lifting both hands into the air. 'Why has it gone?' I asked, intrigued to know if he had a reason. 'I am one monk,' replied Osel in all seriousness.

Then I asked it: 'Are you Lama Yeshe?'; Osel: 'No, I am Tenzin Osel.' Then he paused for some long seconds, thinking, formulating words. 'Before, I am Lama Yeshe. Now Tenzin Osel, one monk.'

Osel had said it, and said it in such a way that it was clear it was not some pat formula that others had instructed him in. I knew for a fact that Basili, David and the family *never* indoctrinated him in this way, wanting as much as anyone for him to reveal who he was himself. This statement had come direct from his own mind.

The future of Lama Tenzin Osel Rinpoche, to give him his proper title, remains to be formulated. As Basili and other western and Tibetan monks at Kopan agree, no one is quite sure what to do with him. There is no precedent among the Tibetan Buddhist hierarchy for one such as he. In one sense he's a recognized Tibetan lama, in another he's made it clear by his birth that he's thrown tradition aside. Already there are some gentle disputes as to whether they are doing the right things with him. Some feel he should be more isolated from the stream of visitors coming to see him, not play so much and be channelled into more religious activities befitting his status. 'The problem is he is so young. Most Tibetan rinpoches don't come to monasteries until they are four or five. We are all really having to feel our way,' said Basili.

For now the plans that the Dalai Lama and Lama Zopa laid down are still being taken as the prototype. In the next year a house will be built for him within the grounds of the new Sera monastery, near Mysore, in southern India. It will be large enough to contain Osel, three attendants (English-, Spanish- and Tibetan-speaking), a permanent spiritual master for Osel, Lama Zopa, when he's free to stay, and selected western visitors. There, at Sera, Osel will begin his Buddhist studies in earnest, receiving teachings, learning texts, practising debate, doing retreat and developing his own spiritual practice. He will be there 10 or 15 years, it is thought, which will be much shorter than the education of Tibetan geshes who usually do not finish their studies until they are over 30. As Lama Zopa says, he needs to have a solid foundation of Buddhist philosophy and meditation. For Osel it should not be so much a matter of learning, more of remembering, and the process will therefore be much quicker for him than for others.

The family will not be going with him. They've accepted the fact calmly and even with some enthusiasm. 'I think it's good he goes there. He needs to know *everything*, the whole thing. Besides in Sera he will have more space, which he needs in order to grow. Now at Kopan I feel he is not alone enough, he always has people with him, wanting things from him,' said Maria.

But as the special education of Osel demands he will not disappear totally for all these years. Throughout his Tibetan spiritual training he will maintain his contact and continuity with the West. This will be achieved partly through having western attendants with him permanently, reminding him of his own culture and roots, and partly through regular visits to the West. There are plans that at some time he will complement his Buddhist studies with a modern western education, particularly in the sciences and mathematics. This way it is hoped he will be able to speak the language of physics and chemistry and instil into it the profound wisdom of the mind. In such a way he will truly continue the great work of Lama Yeshe, bridging the divide between East and West, seeking and expounding the truth of the universality of all things.

That, at least, is the plan. Whether Osel will have the means or the will to fulfil all that is expected of him remains to be seen. How he will grow is a drama yet to be presented to us. For some, particularly the monks, the sooner Osel starts revealing himself as a lama the happier they will be. For them the proof of his reincarnation will be when he starts performing the actions of a highly realized, fully endowed traditional Tibetan spiritual master. 'I can't judge if he's a Buddha or not – but we need to put him into a good environment and give him the best education to help him become the great teacher and communicator he was in his past life,' said Basili, echoing what many ordained men and women feel.

For others, including his parents, holiness does not necessarily have to manifest in saying prayers and mantras. Maria and Paco are even prepared for him to abandon his robes when he is an adult, and fulfil some other role outside the monastic one. 'It's possible he may never be a lama with a mala,' said Maria. 'Personally I don't think he will be conventional, but it doesn't matter. Lama Yeshe wasn't conventional either.

'And I see Osel becoming more and more like Lama Yeshe every day! I once remember Lama Yeshe turning up in Italy wearing Moroccan clothes and a big hat. He broke everybody's ideas, conceptions. You see what he was trying to do was open the eyes, the ears, the mind. This kind of energy Lama Osel is showing increasingly. When you try to get him to say a mantra he gabbles some nonsense. He doesn't want to be anyone's puppet! And so already he too is destroying all the expectations people have about how he should behave. But when he thinks you are not looking and he sees a dying insect, then he will go over to it, blow on it and say mantras to it under his breath. He will do it of his own accord, not in order to put on a show.'

That too is completely in keeping. For didn't Lama Yeshe say over and over again that saying mantras, performing the outer ritual of Tibetan Buddhism was not what it was all about? For Lama Yeshe, understanding the workings of the human mind, going to the essence of all religions, transmitting kindness and developing the good heart were the essentials of any spiritual path.

Maria continued: 'For me the purpose of Lama Osel's life is to finish the job started by Lama Yeshe. Lama Yeshe couldn't help westerners as much as he wanted because he was limited by his Tibetanness. He chose to be reborn in a way where he could work more effectively. With the background of Tibetan wisdom and western science I believe he will truly be able to reach people. I can imagine him talking at large gatherings and his message will still be the same: "Please stop suffering – you are completely crazy! You are caught up in this mad scene and don't know how to stop." And like before, he will begin to show people the way out. For me Osel has the same mind as Lama Yeshe, and he will follow the same trajectory. Whatever he does will be for the benefit of others.'

All this is speculation. For all we know Osel may turn out to be another Krishnamurti (the Indian sage who rejected the role of the new Messiah that was given to him by the eager group of theosophists who found and trained him since childhood). But if the marriage of East and West is to be consummated in Osel, then the future promises to be exciting indeed. The combination of the West's scientific expertise, gained from exploring external phenomena, together with the East's profound knowledge of the nature of reality, including man's heart, gleaned from centuries of looking inwards, could be electric, and the most adventurous leap forward in humankind's evolution. The mending of the world. It is a move which the Dalai Lama, who receives delegations of scientists eager to exchange views on subjects such as the nature of the mind, is only too keen to propagate.

One thing is certain. Whatever Osel does in the future the world will be ready, waiting. For such is his unique destiny that his presence has been established since birth, and his credentials fixed. Whatever path he takes, he will need no introductions. The stage is already set.

When I left Kopan Osel came down to the monastery steps to say goodbye. I told him I was getting on a plane but hoped to see him again soon. 'I, too, am going on a plane – far, far away,' he said, pointing to the distant horizon. 'Soon. To a big house with many cows and water.' Those around him looked surprised. No plans were afoot for such a journey, but Osel spoke with such conviction that I took note.

As the taxi pulled away I turned round and saw the small sturdy little boy in the maroon and gold robes waving. It struck me then that perhaps it is not what he does that is the issue but the fact that he *is*.

GLOSSARY

Bell – ritual implement symbolizing emptiness, the ultimate wisdom, the true nature of existence.

Bodhicitta (pronounced bodhichitta) – the altruistic attitude that wishes to release all beings from suffering.

Bodhisattva – someone who is working for enlightenment for the sole purpose of liberating all sentient beings.

Buddha – an awakened one, a fully enlightened being; one who has overcome all obstacles of mind and has realized omniscience together with ultimate compassion.

Chenrezig (Sanskrit *Avalokiteshvara*) – a deity, an emanation of the Buddha personifying universal compassion.

Compassion – the wish that all beings be free from their suffering.

Dharma – spiritual teachings; the spiritual path, 'the way'.

Dorje (pronounced dorjay) – small, ritual implement, consisting of a five-spoked sceptre, symbolizing compassion.

Eightfold path – the Buddhist code of morality covering body, speech and mind: right speech, right action, right livelihood, right effort, right mindfulness, right concentration, right view, right intention.

Emptiness (Sanskrit *Shunyata*) – the actual way in which all things exist; refutation of the apparent independent self-existence of all phenomena; voidness.

Enlightenment – Buddahood.

Equanimity – an attitude that does not distinguish between friend, enemy and stranger, but feels well disposed towards all. The first step in developing *bobhicitta*.

Four noble truths – the theme of Shakyamuni Buddha's teachings as presented in his first discourse: the noble truths of suffering, the cause of suffering, the cessation of suffering and the path leading to the cessation of suffering.

Gelugpa – one of the four sects of Tibetan Buddhism, also known as the yellow hat sect, founded by the 15th-century reformer Je Tsong Khapa.

Geshe – a title indicating completion of the traditional monastic education, equivalent to Doctor of Divinity.

Gompa – monastery, temple.

Heruka – male meditational deity of highest yoga tantra.

Incarnate lama – highly evolved spiritual being who has deliberately taken birth in order to help all living things.

Initiation – empowerment allowing one to receive and practise tantric teachings.

Kalachakra – literally 'Wheel of Time' – advanced Mahayana teachings and meditation.

Karma – literally 'action'. The philosophy of cause and effect – that every action of body, speech and mind carries a result, specifically as imprints on consciousness.

Lama – spiritual guide and teacher.

Lam Rim – a text composed by Je Tsong Khapa delineating the steps on the path to enlightenment.

Mahamudra – literally 'Great Seal' – advanced Mahayana teachings and meditation.

Mahayana – title referring to the northern schools of Buddhism and characterized by the bodhisattva ideal. The 'Great Vehicle'.

Mandala – a diagram symbolic of the entire universe, often used for meditational practice.

Manjushri – deity, an emanation of the Buddha symbolizing fully enlightened wisdom.

Mantra – sacred words of power, usually Sanskrit.

Meditation – the act of 'thinking inwards', becoming fully acquainted with the object of meditation, through both analytical investigation and single-pointed concentration.

Nihilism – the mistaken view that confuses emptiness with nothingness.

Nirvana – the state beyond sorrow and suffering; freedom from karma.

Osel – 'clear light', i.e. the purest state of mind/consciousness.

Osel-Ling – 'place of clear light'.

Puja – religious service, offering ceremony.

Rinpoche – (pronounced Rinposhay) – 'Precious One'; an incarnate lama.

Saddhu – wandering Indian ascetic.

Samsara – cyclic existence; the involuntary recurring cycle of birth and death controlled by ignorance not understanding the true nature of reality.

Shakyamuni Buddha – Gautama Buddha, the historical Buddha who lived in India during the sixth century BC; the fourth of the thousand Buddhas of this present aeon.

Shunyata – emptiness, void.

Stupa – monument housing a relic and symbolizing the divine mind of enlightened beings.

Tantra – the advanced teachings and practices of Buddhism, available only after initiation, the fastest path to enlightenment.

Tenzin – 'holder of the teachings'.

Vajrapani – Tantric deity symbolizing the all-powerful mind of enlightenment.

Yeshe (pronounced yeshey) – 'wisdom'.

Yoga – spiritual practice to develop full integration of body and mind.

Yogi (Sanskrit) – a spiritual practitioner and adept.

Zopa – 'patience'.